Co

MW00626600

Singletrack Rides

Miscellaneous Rides

Acknowledgments

Many years have gone into the writing of this book. Along the way, many miles of trail have been explored and many individuals have provided their inestimable advice, assistance and information. The thought of writing this book was born soon after I arrived on Florida's west coast (in 1997). At the time, most of my motivation stemmed from recent efforts in writing my first book, the Guide to South Florida Off-Road Bicycling. As with the South Florida Guide, the desire to explore a region by bike and then describe the adventures by writing got the best of me.

The writing of this book has progressed in an uneven fashion over the years due to the inescapable intrusion of other priorities like college, travel, several moves, etc. Sometimes months would pass without working on the Guide while other times it seemed like writing (and map making) was all I was doing! A desire to finish the book sooner and to facilitate future marketing, prompted me to invite a close friend, Raymond "Rudy" Miller, on board to help out. Rudy and I have ridden together all over the southeast and worked together for several years as directors of the now defunct Florida Off-Road Bicycle Association (FORBA). I knew how much Rudy liked to ride as well as write, thus he was the most obvious person for the job. He joined me as a co-author in early 2001 and since then has been an invaluable asset in the creation of this book.

Many individuals who helped with the South Florida Guide also helped with this book. I thank Lys Burden, Herb Hiller, Leigh Brooks and Bruce Martin for their continued advice and assistance.

Rebecca Tharrington deserves a paragraph all her own for her skillful editing of the guide and for her tireless picture taking on many long adventures.

Thanks to Glanzer Press for their friendly professionalism and overall adroit guidance.

Others deserving thanks include: my mother Carol Maietta, father Robert DeGraaf, grandfather Howard Hyer, Dan Hyer, Damian Massey, Sam Evans, Buddy & Paula Baker for their publishing knowledge, Kathy Kantaras and Ryan Hendren for their various GIS assistance, Larry Zullo, Dave Smith and perhaps others who I've "temporarily" forgotten.

Rudy wishes to thank his wife, Jean Miller for her encouragement during his frequent absences on countless adventures.

Several mountain bike clubs, namely the hard working volunteers comprising those clubs, deserve thanks for putting in countless hours of trail advocacy, education, creation, design and maintenance. These include: Tampa's SWAMP (Southwest Assoc. of Mountain bike Pedalers) and the WTA (Wilderness Trails Assoc.), Lakeland's RRMBA (Ridge Riders Mountain Bike Assoc.), Ocala's OMBA (Ocala Mountain Bike Assoc.), and the Florida Freewheelers. Others fitting this mold that deserve to be acknowledged include: Dan Andrews and crew of D&S Cycling Center, Sebring, for their efforts at Sun-N-Lakes Preserve, the Gone Riding folks at Hard Rock and Reddick, and those anonymous riders responsible for the North Port Trail. Thanks also to those bike shops who support the trails. Without bike shops and knowledgeable staff we'd all be lost.

Each federal, state and local land managing agency listed in the Guide is to be thanked for providing assistance, map usage (when applicable), etc., along the way. These folks know who they are and, unfortunately, are too numerous to list individually.

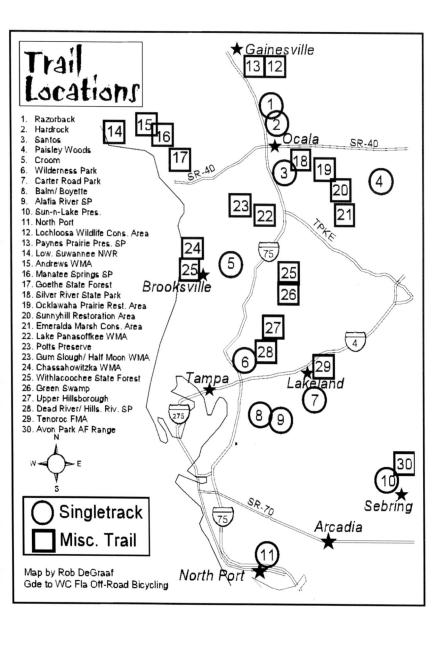

Trail Locations

1. Razorback
2. Hardrock
3. Santos
4. Paisley Woods
5. Croom
6. Wilderness Park
7. Carter Road Park
8. Balm/ Boyette
9. Alafia River SP
10. Sun-n-Lake Pres.
11. North Port
12. Lochloosa Wildlife Cons. Area
13. Paynes Prairie Pres. SP
14. Low. Suwannee NWR
15. Andrews WMA
16. Manatee Springs SP
17. Goethe State Forest
18. Silver River State Park
19. Ocklawaha Prairie Rest. Area
20. Sunnyhill Restoration Area
21. Emeralda Marsh Cons. Area
22. Lake Panasoffkee WMA
23. Potts Preserve
23. Gum Slough/ Half Moon WMA
24. Chassahowitzka WMA
25. Withlacoochee State Forest
26. Green Swamp
27. Upper Hillsborough
28. Dead River/ Hills. Riv. SP
29. Tenoroc FMA
30. Avon Park AF Range

⬭ Singletrack
▢ Misc. Trail

Map by Rob DeGraaf
Gde to WC Fla Off-Road Bicycling

5

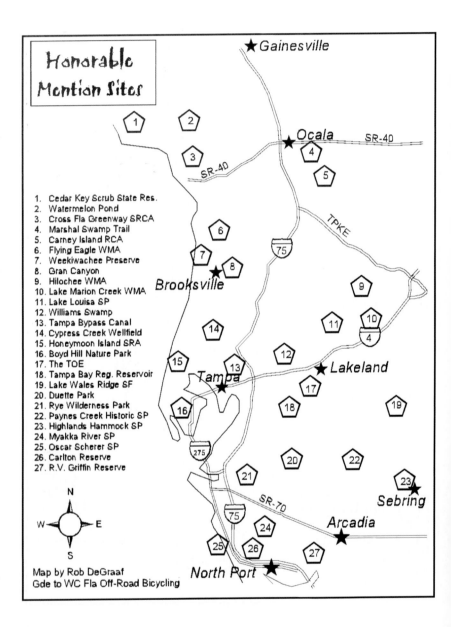

Honorable Mention Sites

★ Gainesville

Ocala ★   SR-40

1. Cedar Key Scrub State Res.
2. Watermelon Pond
3. Cross Fla Greenway SRCA
4. Marshal Swamp Trail
5. Carney Island RCA
6. Flying Eagle WMA
7. Weekiwachee Preserve
8. Gran Canyon
9. Hilochee WMA
10. Lake Marion Creek WMA
11. Lake Louisa SP
12. Williams Swamp
13. Tampa Bypass Canal
14. Cypress Creek Wellfield
15. Honeymoon Island SRA
16. Boyd Hill Nature Park
17. The TOE
18. Tampa Bay Reg. Reservoir
19. Lake Wales Ridge SF
20. Duette Park
21. Rye Wilderness Park
22. Paynes Creek Historic SP
23. Highlands Hammock SP
24. Myakka River SP
25. Oscar Scherer SP
26. Carlton Reserve
27. R.V. Griffin Reserve

Brooksville

Lakeland ★

Tampa ★

Sebring ★

Arcadia ★

North Port ★

Map by Rob DeGraaf
Gde to WC Fla Off-Road Bicycling

6

Introduction

For its size, west-central Florida is overflowing with great off-road bicycling trails. And, as the popularity of mountain-biking continues to increase in Florida, so do the opportunities for riding. On the rise are offers from land managers to design and construct new trails. This pattern is being repeated throughout the state and is exemplified in west-central Florida.

Sharing Trail with Vehicles?

We decided early on to include very few off-road trails and dirt roads that permit motor-vehicle use. We believe that one of the things off-road bicyclists strive to distance themselves from is the "roads" themselves, and the vehicular use found on those roads. The only rides included that are shared with vehicles are those which afford exceptional or unique natural attributes for their region. These also have minimal or seasonal vehicular use and enforced slow speed limits. In our opinion, the natural quality and scenery found along these dirt roads and trails overrides occasional vehicle contact.

Why are Some Trails Missing? A Cause for Advocacy

Most of the singletrack trails in west-central Florida have been included in this guide. However, there are a couple that have been left out. There is a good reason for this. The effect and purpose of a guidebook is to lead people to the places within. Thus, by omitting unapproved or rebel trails, we are choosing to direct cyclists to trails which were "legally" constructed. At approved sites, permission to build trail was granted to clubs and/ or individuals by land managers or land owners. This is the ideal situation for a mountain bike trail.

With the recent destruction of lands housing the famous K-mart Trail in West Palm Beach, Florida, we were all painfully reminded of the ephemeral nature of unapproved trails. Local mountain bikers in that region (including myself) became spoiled by having the extra ride site virtually in our backyards. We bought our time, but then came the bulldozers. After years of rumors portending site development, the woods were finally cleared early in 2001 to make way for yet one more (unneeded) strip mall. We will all miss that trail yet at the same time should learn from this example by making every attempt to build trails at approved sites. Without doing so we risk several things: 1. Losing the site to development, 2. Increased contempt and worsened reputation toward mountain bikers, and 3. Losing access for other reasons like that of private ownership (leading to #1 above).

Many cyclists ride the sites listed in this guide on a frequent basis yet do little when it comes to trail work and advocacy (many thanks to those who have helped on the trails)! It seems that we find it easy to "make time" to ride - therefore "making time" to put back into our trails the enjoyment we take from them should not be any harder.

For local advocacy efforts we recommend contacting any of the following: your local off-road bicycling club, park management, county commissioners, county bicycle coordinators, or the Florida Bicycle Association. These sources should serve as a guide for attempting to gain access on any property. The International Mountain Bicycling Association (IMBA) can also provide guidance concerning establishing a mountain-bike club (see contact information in this section). Speaking with the land manager of a given site is typically the first step in advocating for off-road bike trails. Do you know of a property that you think would make for good bike trails? Then simply call or visit the site to get more information and also to mention your interests in being able to ride your bicycle on off-road trails at that site.

A Subject of Difficulty

"Difficulty Measure" -- The difficulty percentages for each trail are subjective: These are our own behind-the-handlebars opinions regarding a particular trail's overall difficulty and/ or level of technicality. Each percentage represents our opinion of the overall amount of trail at each site that could be labeled as "beginner," "intermediate," or "advanced."

Navigating Tips & Geography 101

On large or especially remote sites, we suggest using a Global Positioning System (GPS) if you have one. Rob uses a Garmin GPS II+ attached to his handlebars with a Garmin mount. A GPS is useful for several reasons:

1. You can obtain your true location in latitude/ longitude coordinates then compare this to a map which has GPS grids (e.g., a USGS topo quad). This will show you where you are on the map. Note that basic maps do not typically have GPS grids on them, so be sure to obtain those that do!

2. Most GPS devices create an "electronic breadcrumb" trail as you move across the land (or water). This trail is drawn on the GPS and can be used as a navigational aid. Basically it shows where you've been. It then becomes very easy to retrace your route back by following the same trail on the GPS. This can be "very" helpful on epic rides on huge tracts of wilderness where you made dozens of turns. In the making of my books, my GPS has become my navigational best friend!

A big warning, however, is that you should always back up a GPS with a compass and a quality map such as a USGS topographic map, Digital Orthophotographic Quad (DOQ - this is an aerial map) or perhaps one included in this Guide. Dropping your GPS in the swamp or bashing it on a tree may prematurely end its life. You better have backup in case this happens. You should also work on basic navigational skills, using a map and compass, understanding map scale, legends, declination (when needed), etc. Learn how to take a bearing using a compass, and know how to use this skill in the woods (e.g., retracing your route).

Also, when comparing your GPS coordinates with those on a map, make sure that both devices are in the same coordinate system (datum)! This is vital as there are several different "projections" of the earth meaning that all maps are not created equal. For example, if your GPS is set at WGS 84 datum, be sure your map was created using this datum. Otherwise, finding your true location on a map may not be possible. First, look on your map to see what datum it is. Then, if necessary, adjust your GPS datum accordingly. This is not very difficult in most of the units I've used.

Common sense is key. When planning a ride, don't bite off more than you can chew. How much time do you have for the ride? Have you or anyone else you know ridden the planned trail? Take mental notes and mental pictures while you're pedaling. Turn around and look at trail intersections and other landmarks to aid your memory for the return trip (i.e., if you're heading back that way). Things look different from different angles. There have been times when I've left a stick or other object at an intersection, pointing toward the way I came from, in order to retrace my route back.

Using the sun can be helpful depending on time of day. However, this becomes much less effective mid-day, and somewhat tricky in certain seasons when the sun is not directly east or west or on extremely overcast days. Bringing a reliable, name brand compass will save you many headaches in the back country. Last but certainly not least, tell someone where you're going and what time/ date you expect to be back. Even if you're not riding alone, it's still a safe measure to inform someone outside your group of your trip plan.

FBA/ FORBA

A portion of the proceeds from sales of this guide will be donated to the Florida Bicycle Association (FBA), for use in continued efforts toward advocacy and development of new trails on existing and potential lands and toward maintenance and responsible use of our existing trails. FORBA (Florida Off-Road Bicycle Advocates) is an advisory board to the FBA and addresses statewide off-road cycling issues. FBA provides a unified voice for off-road cyclists and works behind the scenes "politically" to strive for equal access to lands for off-road bicycling. FBA can also assist local clubs in trail-building efforts. Individual annual membership is $20. Club membership is $100. Quarterly newsletters for members. Contact the FBA on the web at: www.flbicycle.org Email: fba@flbicycle.org

IMBA

The International Mountain Bicycling Association is a non-profit organization that educates cyclists, advocates for access rights, and helps to advance a positive image of the sport. To contact IMBA call (303)-545-9026, or email at IMBA@aol.com. Their website is http://www.imba.com; and their mailing address is PO Box 7578, Boulder, CO 80306.

IMBA's Rules of the Trails

Ride on open trails only. Riding closed trails hurts mountain biking's image and can result in greater restrictions on all cyclists. Also, do not ride on wet trails, as doing so contributes to erosion.

Leave no trace. Don't litter. Pack out more than you pack in, and leave trails better than you found them. An extra moment of care will keep the great outdoors great!

Control your bicycle. Don't skid. Skidding is unsafe, and it can degrade the surface of the trail.

Always yield trail. When approaching hikers or runners, slow down, prepare to stop, establish communication, and wait to pass safely. When passing equestrians, use extra caution: be ready to dismount and ask the horseback rider for instructions.

Plan ahead. Carry a spare tube and pump, tools, food, water, and a small first aid kit. Also, tell someone where you are going and when you expect to return, just in case. Remember to always wear a helmet.

Never scare animals. Respect wildlife, livestock, and pets. Give them plenty of space.

IMBA's 20-20-20 Vision

IMBA promotes a plan, called the 20-20-20 Vision, that calls for cyclists to join their local club (typical cost: $20), to join IMBA ($20), and to work on or for trails (20 hours a year). We as off-road bicyclists should become more involved in our local trails by taking part in this "vision."

Honorable Mention Sites

These trails vary in level of quality. Many came close to receiving a full writeup, map, and photo while others barely deserve honorable mention. Many have been included because they provide a quality nature experience and may be enjoyable to the open-minded and adventurous off-road cyclist looking to ride as many different trails as possible. Some of these sites are worth a separate trip while others should only be visited if you're already in the area. Be sure to call before heading out as some of these trails, like others in the Guide, have unusual days and hours of operation.

Rudy Miller and I have done our best to paint a picture as to why a trail received honorable mention versus complete coverage. This section will be changed and updated on a regular basis. Many hours of literature research and countless hours of pedaling went into this section. Basically, no stone was left unturned regarding potential places to bike off-road. However, there is a slight chance we may have missed something: So, if you know of an approved off-road trail that we have missed and you feel it is worthy of inclusion, please contact us. We will go explore!

Northern Section

Carney Island Recreation and Conservation Area: 685 acres. This is a small Marion County park located southeast of Belleview near Ocklawaha. Main numbers: (352) 288-8999 and 236-7111. From the light on CR-25 in Ocklawaha, travel west 1.5 miles and turn south as indicated by the park sign. 7/10 mile down this road is a stop sign. The park entrance is straight ahead. Almost surrounded by Lake Weir on the east and Little Lake on the west, the park offers 4.5 miles of trail for hikers and bikers. Horses and vehicles not permitted. The level, graded trail has gentle curves and forms a huge loop with numerous connecting trails in the middle. Foliage is so dense and the old live oaks so enormous that the trail views are almost enchanted. A fox crossed the trail in front of me, stopped, and casually watched me over his shoulder. A snake slither track crossed the sand trail leaving a mark almost 5 inches wide. The trails closest to the parking areas are great for beginners. Conversely, about 2 inches of soft sand on the trails furthest from the parking areas are likely to be the nemesis of inexperienced riders. There are rest rooms along the trail and a sandy beach and swimming area near the parking at Little Lake. Small entrance fee.

Cedar Key Scrub State Reserve: 4,988 acres. Levy County. Managed by Florida Department of Environmental Protection, Division of Recreation and Parks. Main number: (352) 543-5567. Access is from US-19/ 98 near Chiefland. Two separate tracts. Western tract is located on CR-347. SR-24 intersects 347 a couple miles west of the first tract described above. Head north on 347 appx. 1 ½ miles. Trailhead is on west side of road. Riding in this section is better than in the eastern tract. More mileage is hardpack, routes are longer and more shade can be found. Trail 6 is main loop, 8 is a very scenic out-and-back, 7 and 10 are nice. Eastern tract is located 15 miles west of US-19 on SR-24. Trailhead on north side of road. Several dirt roads in this tract were pretty soft at time of writing, however, a recent prescribed fire had been conducted prior to my visit. Heavy trucks and machinery used for the fire may have loosened the roads up more than normal. This is my theory anyhow. Either way, expect some sand in this section! Trails 2, 5 and 3 form a loop. . . . Bald eagle overhead at trailhead! Gopher tortoise, scrub jay, swallow-tailed kite, grey fox, white-tail deer, etc. Slash & sand pine, wax myrtle, scrub oak, blackberry, palmetto, cabbage palm, and a reclusive cedar. Don't miss nearby town of Cedar Key. Camping at County Shell Mound Park, north on 347 to 326, almost to end of road. Other nearby "full" writeups in Guide: Andrews WMA, Lower Suwannee NWR, and Manatee Springs SP.

<u>Cross Florida Greenway State Recreation and Conservation Area</u>: 81,290 acres. Citrus, Levy, Marion and Putnam counties. Multi trailheads. Managed by Florida Department of Environmental Protection, Office of Greenways and Trails (OGT) and U.S. Army Corps of Engineers. OGT main number: (877) 822-5208; Ocala Office: (352) 236-7143. Totaling 110 miles in length, this property was originally set aside for the Cross-Florida Barge Canal. Envisioned in the late 1800's, started in 1935 and nixed by Nixon in the late 60's, the canal has gone through many phases of development. Lawsuits filed against the project spoke of serious environmental concerns regarding potential harm to the Floridan Aquifer lying just below the surface of the planned deep canal. Fresh water could accidentally discharge and salt water could unintentionally seep in. In 1990 the project was officially de-authorized and the wheels of today's conservation efforts began to spin. . . The property stretches from Yankeetown on the Gulf to the Rodman Reservoir in Putnam County. The most established and most popular bike trails are found in Santos (see Santos Trail under Singletrack rides). . . Another trailhead is at Inglis Island, which lies between the lock and the main spillway, off US-19in Inglis. Take W. Riverwood Dr. to the parking area at dam. Two to three miles of unpaved trails are found on the north side of dam. Nice views of Lake Rousseau from here as well.

<u>Flying Eagle Wildlife Management Area</u>: 10,950 acres. Citrus County. Co-managed by Southwest Florida Water Management District (800-423-1476) and Florida Fish and Wildlife Conservation Commission (850-488-4676). Access is from US-41 near Inverness and Floral City. Take Eden Dr. east from US-41. Eden Dr. becomes Moccasin Slough Rd. Drive 4 ½ miles to parking area/ gate. Thirteen miles of dirt roads open for off-road bicycling. Conditions range from shady hard-pack to long, open sugar sand stretches. In general, the best cycling is along the Loop Road and an unnamed road in southern section of property. These two trails have ample tree canopy, hardpack conditions, and a tiny bit of elevation change. Most of the Main Road and sections of the Dike Road are soft sugar sand. Many other trails nearby. See this section and rest of Guide.

<u>Marshal Swamp Trail</u>: Marion County. Managed by Florida Department of Environmental Protection, Office of Greenways and Trails (OGT), Ocala Office: (352) 236-7143. This trail is east of Ocala, about a mile south of Silver River State Park. From SR-40 in Silver Springs go south on SR-35 1 ½ miles and turn left onto 7th. 4 ½ miles later there is a trailhead on your right behind the Greenways office.

The trail leads through the swamp on a twisted course covered with loose gravel. Until this surface gets worn in, the gravel will continue to make noise under your tires, warning the world of your approach, and increasing the difficulty of bicycle control. There are numerous wooden bridges over wet areas and during high rains, much of the trail may be under water. The trail goes out and back a distance of three miles each way.

Watermelon Pond: Levy County. At time of writing, this site was in the proposal stages. Adjacent to and managed by Goethe State Forest, near Bronson. The Forestry Service is working on a management plan for the site, which boasts old limerock quarries, sinkholes, hardwood forest, scrub and pine flatwoods. Myriad fern, sumac, turkey oak, scrub rosemary and blackberry also prevalent. The terrain sounds very alluring indeed. If you're interested in finding out more and maybe helping with trails in the future, contact: Ernie Ash, Forestry Resource Administrator, at: (352) 955-2238. Ernie's a mountain-biker so give him a call!

Central Section

Boyd Hill Nature Park: 245 acres. Managed by the City of St. Petersburg: (727) 893-7326. From I-275 in St. Pete take exit 4 (54th Ave. South). Head east on 54th Ave. to 9th Street. Make left on 9th then head north to Country Club Way South. Nature Center on right and entrance at gate #2. You will not find much off-road bicycling here, just a couple sections of very short dirt roads scattered amongst 3 miles of paved trails. While small, the park is listed here due to a severe lack of off-road ride sites in St. Pete. If we've missed something, contact us ASAP! Rob used to ride his mtn-bike here from north St. Pete years ago. Combining a road ride with an end goal like Boyd Hill makes sense as it affords increased mileage as well as a scenic turn-around point. The park is shady and has a wide diversity in flora and fauna (some endangered). Adjoining Lake Maggiore, Boyd Hill is among the region's last remaining green spaces. Good family outing/ picnic location. Yield trail to those on foot (more common than bikes).

Cypress Creek Wellfield: 7,400 acres. Pasco County. Managed by Southwest Florida Water Management District (SWFWMD): (800) 423-1476. Both access points located off CR-583 (Ehren Cutoff Rd.). Near Land O Lakes. Main trailhead is at end of Pump Station Rd. past first gate and pump station. Access in the south is from Parkway Blvd., appx. 1.5 miles SE from 583. Contact SWFWMD for a Recreational Guide to District Lands. A trail map is in the Guide. Appx. 5 miles total, unpaved mileage. Several nice, hardpack, doubletrack trails branch off of the main, paved, shared use trail on the property. Pine flatwoods/ palmetto mixed with hardwood (cypress) swamp. Combining unpaved with paved trails is the best way to see more land and gain more mileage. Don't miss the dirt road loop near the flood control structure. Head in from Pumphouse Rd. trailhead looking on your left. Turn into woods before the structure. Trail heads north then back south to paved trail, ending on other side of structure. All trails can be ridden in any direction. In my visits I've seen dozens of wild turkey, many whitetail deer, gopher tortoise, myriad birds, etc.

Gran Canyon: Hernando County. Privately owned. Main number: (352) 796-8955. To reach the park, go west on SR-50 from I-75 exit #301 several miles to the first light. Turn right onto Mondon Hill Rd. proceeding north. After the hill the road heads west. A quarter mile after the curve, take the first paved road to the right (Cooper Terr.) and turn into the first driveway on the right. Park near the big oak tree where you register. Helmets required. The name alone evokes visions of steep, rocky terrain with extended climbs and fast descents. There was a time when this private mountain biking park in an old strip mine had even skilled riders checking their brakes and thinking twice. Trails were narrow, challenging and had a mostly smooth, fast, hard surface. But this changed in the summer of 2001 when the owner closed the park for several months. When it reopened in October, half the trails were still buried beneath several feet of weeds. The other half of the trails had been mowed with a tractor and bush-hog. The wide, dense grass and weed base was most uninviting. The park is being included in this book because we know the place has potential and the owner, John Benefield, assures us that the trails will be groomed by race season. Historically, riding here has only been offered on weekends. We each paid a small fee for a Saturday ride and our group left after riding only 2 ½ miles of the approximately 6 miles that were once available. Call before you go to insure the trails are open and to ascertain overall trail conditions.

Hilochee Wildlife Management Area: 4,922 acres. Lake County. Managed by Florida Fish & Wildlife Conservation Commission, (352) 241-8501 or (850) 488-4676. Like most WMAs, hunting is the apparent focus on Hilochee. However, when I biked here in October, other passive users had signed in at various trailheads: hikers, runners, etc. Didn't see that any had been out biking though. Overall, very few people visit the property. The best riding was on Riddick Grove Road, accessed from US-27, appx. 3.5 miles north of CR-474. At that distance, watch for trailhead and sign on left (west) side of 27. Here you'll find a scenic, hardpack (clay & shell) doubletrack trail heading west appx. 3 mi. before it ends. Head back the same way (let me know if you find any loop options here). Citrus trees intermingle with replanted slash and sand pine forest. This was the largest replanted sand pine forest I had yet seen in FL. Rolling topography, open prairie and wetland terrain are also found. . . The trailhead on CR-474 is approximately 2 1/4 mi. west of US-27. Park headquarters is ½ mi. further west on Yancey Rd. The doubletrack trail from 474 heads north briefly then splits. Left route heads NW appx. 1 mi. before becoming very overgrown. Several equally overgrown spur trails were observed but not explored from the main trail. Ask staff before venturing too far. Right turn at split quickly ends at gate marking property boundary. . . Don't bother with trail in SW section of property. Trail heads south appx. 1000 ft. then ends abruptly. . . The Sand Mine Trailhead from Green Swamp Rd. is accessible by 4WD vehicles only. However, it's barely worth the effort. Open, rolling, sandy, reclaimed agricultural terrain is hot and somewhat mundane. Ride here only for variation or to try to link together other routes. If you do so, bring plenty of water and other vital supplies as it's remote and rugged. Check in with the park as well.

Honeymoon Island State Recreation Area: 385 acres uplands, 2,400 submerged. Pinellas County. Managed by Florida Department of Environmental Protection, Division of Recreation and Parks. Main number: (727) 469-5942. Accessed from US-19 near Clearwater. Take CR-586 west through Dunedin. 586 becomes Causeway Blvd. Follow road across bridge into park. 2.4 miles of trail in varying condition head north through virgin slash pine forest, sea grape, sabal palm and prickly pear cactus. Two trails, Pelican Cove and Osprey, form parallel loops. Expect semi-long sugar sand stretches in a few areas. Trails here are worth riding only if in the area or if wanting to spend the day at the beach. Request a map at the gate when you pay your entrance fee. Local history as rich as island wildlife: Tocobaga Indian settlement as late as the 1500s, "attempted" hog farming in the late 1800s, and a 1921 hurricane which split the island in two – forming Caladesi Island (State Park) to the south (see Caladesi trails in this Guide). Catch a ferry from Honeymoon Island to Caladesi.

Lake Louisa State Park: 4,372 acres. Polk County. Managed by Florida Department of Environmental Protection, Division of Recreation and Parks. Main number: (352) 394-3969. South of Clermont. Take CR-561 south for 7 miles, then turn east on Lake Nellie Rd. and head 2 miles to park entrance road. Or take US-27 south from Clermont, 12 miles. Turn west at entrance station and head appx. 2.8 miles to Lake Dixie. At press time, Lake Louisa SP had little if any decent off-road bicycling. Bicycling is permitted on 13 mile horse trail but excessive sugar sand ruins the trip. In 2001, the park was getting a major facelift. Proposed trails (shared use) were underway as were new park roads, etc. These changes are years away yet, but call the park for the latest details and to voice interest in off-road bicycling. Upon my visit they were receptive and open minded regarding mountain biking.

Lake Marion Creek Wildlife Management Area: 8,083 acres. Polk County. Co-managed by Florida Fish and Wildlife Conservation Commission: (863) 648-3205 and South Florida Water Management District (800) 432-2045. Accessed from CR-580, from Haines City. Huckleberry Island trailhead is appx. 6 miles east of Haines City, on north side of 580. Don't waste your time with the sugar sand roads at Snell Creek trailhead. Instead, head to Huckleberry Island Road. This trail is appx. 2 miles each way, with several optional off-shoots. Conditions are hardpack (lots of limerock) doubletrack. The route heads north through several ecosystems including slash pine/ palmetto flatwoods, open prairie, and gorgeous, shady hardwood hammock that's very difficult to leave in the summer! Don't be too dismayed by sugar sand stretches in the north. They soon end and trails beyond are worth the added effort. Abundant wildlife. Kiosk, sign-in sheet and maps at trailhead. No facilities. No fee.

Tampa Bay Regional Reservoir: Appx. 6000 acres. Hillsborough County. Managed by Tampa Bay Water (813) 910-3205, and Southwest Florida Water Management District. (800) 423-1476. Several thousand acres will comprise the actual reservoir, roads and pipelines. The rest is slated for recreation and conservation. Tampa Bay Water and SWFWMD were in the recreational proposal stages at time of writing, yet, a look into the crystal ball yields: an unpaved 9.1 mile interpretive trail, 5.6 mile shared-use paved trail, primitive camping, environmental education center, non-motorized boat access/ launch on the reservoir, wetland enhancement areas and more. With this property now in public ownership, it becomes a vital link between Balm-Boyette Scrub Preserve to the west and Alafia River State Park to the east. These properties now comprise a sizeable chunk of green space. Better still is the fact that they all permit off-road bicycling. A proposed Boyette/ Alafia linkage trail will run just south of the reservoir along an old railway corridor (See also Boyette and Alafia trails in this Guide).

Tampa Bypass Canal: Hillsborough County. Managed by Southwest Florida Water Management District (SWFWMD): (800) 423-1476. The Canal is fourteen miles long, yet, you cannot ride your bike along its entire route. This is mostly due to impediments such as flood control structures and major roads. However, the Hillsborough Greenways Committee has big plans for the Bypass Canal. A shared use trail may eventually connect Trout Creek Park in the north with McKay Bay in the south. This trail may be paved . . . I researched every access point (via bridges) along the Canal and came up with a couple suggested rides/ trailheads. In general, conditions for off-road bicycling are worse in the south and better in the north (i.e., there are fewer obstructions in the north). The trail consists of grass and occasional shell roads. There is very little shade, thus ride when it's cooler! Hours are from sunrise to sunset . . . For now, try these rides:

1. Park at the Temple Terrace Youth Sports Complex on US-301, or on 301 where it crosses the Canal. Ride north from here on either side of the Canal. Fowler Ave. is less than a mile to the north. North of Fowler, the Canal bisects Cow House Creek, then goes under Morris Bridge Rd. You can bike a little further north from here to the Trout Creek Park entrance road (See also Wilderness Park trails). This route is appx. 4 miles round trip. Fowler also has decent access.

2. Also, contact the District at above number to inquire about several short paved trails along the Bypass Canal.

The TOE: Appx. 500 acres. Polk County. Located in Lakeland on private property. The TOE (Trail Of Experience) is certainly among the top cadre of Florida singletrack trails. Moreover, many would agree, myself included, that the well-shaded, moonscape like terrain here affords some of the best, most advanced level riding in the state. Novice riders: forget about it!! Intermediate: find out how good you "really" are. Advanced: bring it on baby! An appx. 8 mile loop existed at time of writing. Several trail sections are optional as are several scattered, wood stunts. Ridge Riders Club members, including myself, have put in many long hours of creative trail design and construction here. The TOE appears in this section of the Guide for two main reasons:

1. It's not open to everyone. Riders must be card carrying members of the Ridge Riders Mountain Biking Assoc. (RRMBA). Membership is $30 per year, including TOE pass. Getting to ride the trail regularly is worth the fee.

2. The property is sadly destined to be developed by appx. 2003 (emphasis on the "appx."). This is first hand information passed on to me by one of the land owners. My suggestion is to join RRMBA and do so ASAP! Otherwise risk hearing, years later, all your buddies describe the killer trails you missed at the TOE. . . . For more info on the TOE contact RRMBA President, Kent Hickman at: (863) 619-5001 or

on the web at: www.ridgeriders.net

Weekiwachee Preserve: 9000 acres. Hernando County. Managed by Southwest Florida Water Management District (SWFWMD): (800) 423-1476. Located near Spring Hill, from US-19, west on CR-595 (Osowaw Blvd.). Trailhead on right. Alternate trailhead on Shoal Line Blvd. The trail is 5.5 miles total, 1.3 miles of this is paved. The unpaved mileage is hard pack lime rock with occasional muddy sections. This is a disturbed piece of land that was originally a lime rock quarry. The deep pits have since filled with clear water creating scenic lakes. Wildlife includes bald eagle, deer, alligator, gopher tortoise and reclusive Florida black bear. Portions of the trail may be closed temporarily in the Spring to protect ground-nesting birds. Minimal shade to be found excepting four rest shelters along the trail. The flat, short trails are excellent for families and beginners but keep a close eye on your children with all the water.

Williams Swamp: Hillsborough County. Also known as the Dover Fishing Area, this site is a cooperative effort between Hillsborough County Parks & Recreation and Public Utilities. Main number: (813) 975-2160. Access is from SR-60, east of Brandon and just east of Dover Road. An appx.. 5 mile loop comprised of levees and other trails can be ridden from here either to the east or the north. Trail is not marked and is tricky to follow in sections, however, with some exploring, finding one's way back onto the main loop is not difficult. Don't be too dismayed by sugar sand which you'll find in a few sections. It makes up for a relatively small percentage of overall mileage. The sand is caused by horses which also share the trail. Heading east from trailhead leads into one such section. This is the worst sand in the whole loop. Once north of here, things improve dramatically. Be courteous to horseback riders. They were here first!... Flora consists of oak, slash pine, gallberry, beautyberry, lantana, pokeweed, rattlebox, muscadine, etc.

Southern Section

Carlton Reserve: 24,565 acres. Managed by Sarasota County Community Services Parks and Recreation. Main number: (941) 486-2547. Located off I-75, exit #193, Jacaranda Blvd. Head east on Jacaranda then right on Border Rd. Left on Mabry Carlton Pkwy. Park entrance on right. All in all, the Carlton family owns a ton of land in south Florida, much of it set aside for conservation. 1.75 miles of unpaved interpretive trail from main parking area. Yet, this is just a small portion of dirt roads/ trails open to off-road bicyclists on the property. Contact the Reserve for a back country permit and map to explore further. Hammock, pine flatwoods, wet prairie, etc. Restrooms, phones, picnic tables and pavilions. Guided tours, hiking, botanical study. White-tail deer, bobcat, gopher tortoise. 147 bird species have been observed (some common, some rare).

Duette Park: 33,000 acres. Managed by Manatee County Parks and Recreation Department. Duette Park phone: (941) 776-2295. County phone: (941) 742-5923. Easiest access is from I-75 at SR-64 (exit 220). Take 64 east 26 miles to left at Duette Rd. Follow Duette Rd. north 6.6 miles to left at Rawls Rd. This leads into park. Duette Park's main function is providing Manatee County's drinking water supply.

This is done via several deep wells that tap into the Floridan Aquifer. Secondary to this use is recreation. Bikes are permitted on every trail in the Park. These trails are multi-use and are open to vehicles, but vehicular use is very light except during hunting season (call the Park for dates). Trail conditions vary greatly: everything from fast, hardpack limerock roads to deep sugar sand. Trail 1 is entirely hardpack and serves as a central spine through the property, connecting to many other trails as well as the Bear Bay Rd. gate in the south. No vehicular access here without first obtaining a permit at main office in north. However, bikes can pass through the Bear Bay Rd. gate . . . Trail 11, beginning at the main office, is also hardpack. Trail 10 is nice, hardpack doubletrack. Best access to 10 is via Power Line trail from Trail 1 (see map). The following trails are either total sugar sand or are interspersed with long sugary sections: 3, 4, 6, 8, 9, and 13 - 16. Note: several trails were unexplored due to being impounded by other, way-too-sugary, access trails! Shade, cooler temperatures and better wildlife observation are found on dawn or dusk rides. Plans are underway to add shell rock to the most if not all deep sugar sand stretches. This will be a big improvement.

Highlands Hammock State Park: Appx. 9000 acres. Highlands County. Managed by Florida Department of Environmental Protection, Division of Recreation and Parks. Main number: (863) 386-6094. Located on Hammock Road (SR 634), just west of US-27 near Sebring. Appx. eight miles of mostly hardpack roads form a figure-8 pattern and lead through a variety of scenic terrain. Appx. 2 miles of this route is paved. The western portion of the figure-8 is much more shady, thus makes for more enjoyable biking. Don't miss the short out-and-back trail leading to the old dam and bridge over Little Charlie Bowlegs Creek. Opening in 1931, the Park is one of Florida's oldest examples of grassroots environmental advocacy. Myriad wildlife, including many threatened and endangered species such as bald eagle and Florida panther. Other activities include hiking, camping and nature study. Small entrance fee at gate.

Lake Wales Ridge State Forest: 20,242 acres. Polk County. Managed by Florida Division of Forestry. Main number: (863) 635-7801. Two main tracts: Walk-in-the-Water in north and Arbuckle in south. Both are near Lake Wales and Avon Park. Walk-in-the-Water tract accessed from CR-630, appx. 8 miles east of US-27. Turn left onto Walk-in-the-Water Road. Arbuckle tract accessed from 27A, north of Avon Park. Take 27A a few miles north from US-27 then turn right onto Wilson Rd. Follow Wilson several miles then make right onto Lake Arbuckle Rd. Drive appx. 2 miles then turn right onto School Bus Rd . . . There are just a few dirt roads here open to off-road bicycling, probably not worth a separate trip, except maybe for those already in the region and those desiring to study the unique Lake Wales Ridge ecosystem. Roads are shared with vehicles. Arbuckle tract: School Bus Road is 5 - 6 miles long, mostly hardpack, open terrain. (Park HQ on School Bus Rd.). Lake Godwin Rd. is short, hardpack doubletrack leading to scenic Lake Godwin. Cow Pen Road has not fully been explored by the author. Tram Road, in the south, is wheel-sucking sugar sand! Reedy Creek, crossed by School Bus Rd. in the north, makes for a nice stopping point. School Bus Rd. reaches SR-64 in the south but is only accessed by bicycle due to being gated.

Myakka River State Park: 28,875 acres. Sarasota and Manatee Counties. Managed by Florida Department of Environmental Protection, Division of Recreation and Parks. Main number: (941) 361-6511. Located off SR-72, west of Arcadia and east of Sarasota. Exit 205 east from I-75. There are around 53 miles of trail open to cyclists here. Unfortunately, most of this mileage is too sandy unless ridden soon after a rain. I searched high and low for great doubletrack and dirt roads and found just a little of each. Other activities include camping, paddling, fishing, hiking, nature study, etc. Myakka Outpost: bike and canoe rentals: (941) 923-1120. Small entrance fee at gate.

Oscar Scherer State Park: 1,384 acres. Sarasota County. Managed by Florida Department of Environmental Protection, Division of Recreation and Parks. Main number: (941) 483-5956. Located off US-41 near town of Osprey. South of Sarasota. Appx. 16 miles of dirt roads and trails in widely varying condition are open to off-road bicyclists. Some sections are fast hardpack while others are snail-paced sugar sand. Scenery consists of predominantly slash pine and palmetto terrain. Oak hammock and scrub prairie also. Gopher tortoises rule the land! Camping, paddling (on South Creek), hiking, nature study, etc. Small entrance fee at gate.

Paynes Creek Historic State Park: 394 acres. Hardee County. Managed by Florida Department of Environmental Protection, Division of Recreation and Parks. Main number: (863) 375-4717. Located near Bowling Green, a couple miles east of US-17 on SR-664A. The Park is significant in its rich cultural history and in its environmental preservation. In 1849 the Kennedy-Darling Store and Fort Chokonikla were established here as a result of continued friction between the Seminoles and white settlers, who were encroaching on Seminole lands. See the Park's exceptional visitor center to learn more. The appx. 5 miles of mostly shaded, mostly hardpack trail are worth a trip. One trail winds along Paynes Creek, leading to the confluence of the creek and the Peace River. Other trails wind through upland slash pine/ palmetto forest, lead to various historical sites, and cross over the creek on a picturesque suspension bridge. Other activities include picnicking, fishing, hiking, nature and historical study. Small entrance fee at gate.

R.V. Griffin Reserve: 6,000 acres. Desoto County. Managed by Southwest Florida Water Management District (SWFWMD): (800) 423-1476. Located due east of Pt. Charlotte and North Port. Exit 170 on CR-769 (Kings Highway). Head north on 769 for appx. 5 miles. Trailhead and parking on left across from Peace River Water Treatment Plant. At time of writing, kiosk at trailhead was not accurate regarding trails open to off-road bicycling. Contact SWFWMD to obtain a Rec. Guide to WMD lands and to ask about most current bicycle trail information on RV Griffin. This is a diverse property with several agencies making use of land for varied purposes. As such, trail locations and quality are subject to change without notice. The Reserve is shaped like a perfect triangle. Seven miles of trail were open at time of writing, this being located along southern and western edges/ fence lines of triangle, and along a 2-mile, straight, east-west connector trail in the south. Central and northern trail sections not open to cyclists due to property lessee desires.

Call WMD with further questions. A linkage trail between here and the WMD owned Deep Creek property to the south is planned for the future. At time of writing only hiking was available on the latter.

Rye Wilderness Park: 145 acres. Managed by Manatee County Parks and Recreation Department. (941) 776-0900. East of Bradenton. SR-64 east to left on Rye Road. Make right onto Woodstock Road. Various trailheads and short dirt roads on north side of Woodstock Rd. (labeled S-2 thru S-5). Park HQ and most park facilities reached by crossing Manatee River on Rye Rd. heading north. Make first right into park. At press time, trail mileage here was much too small to make worthwhile a separate trip. However, if your bikes are already loaded on car rack or if you're going to be in the area for other riding, Rye may be worth a stop. On a hot summer day, it makes for a decent little picnic spot and there is swimming at a beach near Rye Rd. bridge. Ecologically, Rye is a small yet important link in protecting the upper Manatee River watershed. Myriad wildlife including sand pine scrub community with gopher tortoise, etc. Chance of shell rocking trails in future. This would improve conditions here. Camping, paddling, fishing and hiking available.

Singletrack Rides

Reddick - Razorback

Hardrock

Santos

Ocala NF - Paisley Woods

Withlacoochee State Forest - Croom

Lower Hillsborough Wilderness Park

Carter Road Park

Balm Boyette Scrub Preserve

Alafia River State Park

Sun-n-Lake Preserve

North Port

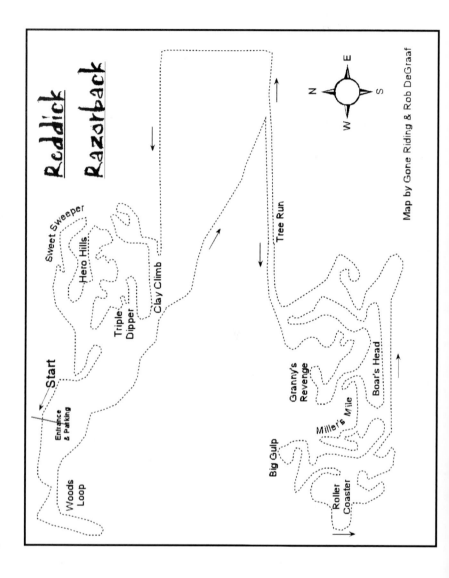

Reddick Razorback

Sweet Sweeper
Hero Hills
Triple Dipper
Clay Climb
Start
Entrance & Parking
Woods Loop
Tree Run
Granny's Revenge
Big Gulp
Miller's Mile
Roller Coaster
Boar's Head

N
E
S
W

Map by Gone Riding & Rob DeGraaf

22

Reddick Mountain Bike Park - Razorback

Location: Just north of Ocala

Managing Agency: Private ownership, managed by Gone Riding

Trail Length: 10 miles

Difficulty: 90% intermediate; 10% advanced

Trail Type: 100% singletrack

Description: Strong and experienced mountain bikers will be hard pressed to find better riding in this part of the state. Trails here are challenging, exhilarating and just plain fun to ride. From the grassy parking area, a one-way trail leads into the woods where the trees almost meet the double track on your right. This first section has many trees to dodge as you spin through continuous curves leading back and forth in a rhythmic pattern. A few minor ups and downs here provide enjoyment, but for the most part, this section serves as a warm up for what's to come.

Things get even more interesting after the first section. Riders are faced with many challenging climbs, tight turns and plenty of steep drops. Big grins begin to appear. While most of the trail surface is smooth, comprised of hard clay and rock, there are plenty of big rocks and roots lying in wait for daydreaming or exhausted riders. Most of the trail is buried in deep shade due to its course winding beneath many huge, grandfather oaks.

One of the great achievements in the design of this trail is the swinging rhythm it imparts to the biker. Abrupt changes are absent. The trail winds around an active mine, providing the source of all the big elevation changes. Only the abandoned sections of the old mining terrain are used for the trail. Other sections wind through narrow tree corridors of huge oaks and other hardwoods with agricultural lands lying on both sides. Few riders can complete a loop at Reddick their first time without dabbing or dismounting, and three loops will whip the zip out of even the strongest riders. If you are an experienced mountain-biker, Reddick is an absolute must.

Wildlife: Because the fields and mine around which these trails loop are actively worked, there is little wildlife other than that found at the after ride parties. There are some interesting birds here, but riders are normally too busy watching the trail to notice them. This is my excuse for not having identified them yet.

Et cetera: Marion County. This is a private park open to members only. A small fee at the gate will get you a membership card and there is an additional small daily use fee. **The trails are only open on weekends and occasional races may close the trails so call before heading out. Call or check on line for a current schedule. Helmets required. Bring plenty of food and water (several bottles and/ or a hydration pack). Also bring a couple of spare tubes, a pump, and vital tools. Mosquitoes can be bothersome during wet weather so be sure to bring repellent.

When to Go: Other than on race days, the park is open every weekend. Clay here is very slick during and immediately after rain. Drier weather equals better riding. However, thanks to the abundant shade, summer riding (if not too wet) is also awesome.

Contacts: Gone Riding: (352) 873-9279. On the web: www.goneriding.com

Directions: From I-75, take exit #358 (CR-326) and head east about a mile. At the traffic light, turn left onto CR-25A. Proceed north appx. 7 miles to traffic light in Reddick. Make right heading east on CR-316 then continue for about 1 mile to the Razorback entrance on your right noted by a small sign under the big trees. Travel down the main dirt road to a "T" and go right to the pay station. Parking is right and left after the pay station.

Hardrock Cycle Park

Location: North of Ocala

Managing Agency: Privately owned

Trail Length: 7 mile loop

Difficulty: 20% beginner; 60% intermediate; 20% advanced

Trail Type: 100% singletrack

Description: Hardrock Cycle Park offers some of the most exciting and challenging off road riding in the State. This privately owned, commercial biking park offers just about everything a serious mountain biker could find in Florida, including a suspension bridge across Horseshoe Lake. The unique terrain offered at Hardrock is the spoils of a mining operation during the Eisenhower era (50's) when Interstate 75 was constructed. Millions of tons of lime-rock were extracted from this quarry and used as the base for the new highway. Heavy machinery once moved mountains of earth to uncover the rock which was then blasted and removed. There are still remnants of the cables, tracks and an inclined tunnel where huge carloads of rock were pulled mechanically up on 60 inch wide, steel tracks (wider than standard railroad). Today, covered by lush vegetation, the original scarring of the land appears as forested hills, rocky cliffs and a peaceful lake. Most of the park's 100 acres are dedicated to mountain biking with a gorgeous 7 mile, singletrack loop that twists and turns as it leads through continually challenging elevation changes. Most of this is through dense vegetation comprised of trees, vines, ferns, flowers and various types of grasses. The trail base is a combination of hardpack lime-rock and clay providing both speed and good traction, except following rain, at which time the trail becomes as slick as a soap bar

The famous suspension bridge is located in the first third of the loop as canyon walls squeeze the trail closer and closer to Horseshoe Lake until the only option left is to cross the water. The bridge was built by former park owners, Sue and Randy Keuntjes, in 1988 as part of their effort to build a national caliber racing facility on the mined land that they had purchased a year earlier. The bridge is more than 200 feet long, six feet wide and has side cables to prevent a biker from taking an unexpected swim. The swaying and bouncing of the span are much less noticeable while scooting across the planks on a mountain bike than when walking across it trying to take photos.

Et cetera: Marion County. Helmets required. Full hook-up camping and primitive camping on site. Hot showers, restrooms and a laundry facility. Also available at the park are mountain bike inner tubes, miscellaneous items and on most weekends there is a food vendor on site. The charge for day use is $5 while over night tent camping is $10 and full hook-up is $20. Weekly and monthly rates are available. About two weekends a year the park is closed to mountain bikers so it is advised to check their web site or call in advance before heading out.

When to Go: Great riding anytime the trail surface is not wet

Contacts: Hardrock Cycle Park: (352) 732-6697.
On the web at: www.hardrockmx.com

Directions: From I-75 take exit #358 (CR-326) and head east about half a mile. At the traffic light, turn right onto CR-25A. Hardrock is 3/4 of a mile south on your left.

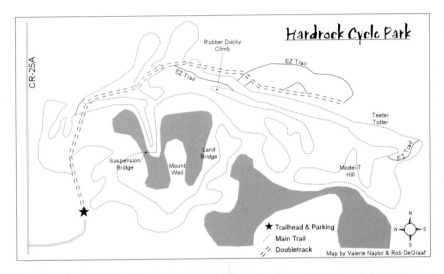

Hard to believe it's Florida. Hardrock suspension bridge.

Photo by Rudy Miller

Santos Trail

Location: Main trailhead in Santos, south of Ocala

Managing Agency: Florida Department of Environmental Protection, Office of Greenways and Trails

Trail Length: Over 60 miles and growing.

Difficulty: 40% beginner, 40% intermediate, 20% advanced

Trail Type: 99% singletrack; 1% doubletrack

Description: If you're a Florida mountain biker and you have not ridden Santos, do the following: 1. Look at yourself in the mirror and ask, "Why?" 2. Next, immediately locate your calendar and look for a day, or better yet, a weekend, not too far off in the future so you can finally get yourself here! The Ocala area is chock full of superb mountain biking (see the many sites listed in this guide). Santos is not only the biggest and oldest of the bunch, it is also the epicenter for most other riding in the region. Spending a long weekend riding Santos and other local Ocala venues is truly a joyous almost religious occasion.

The Ocala Mountain Bike Association (OMBA) has done an amazing job of designing, building, maintaining and integrating trails of varying difficulty into a single location. This "single location" is on property, officially designated as the

Tried to hot-wire it, but it just wouldn't start!   *Photo by Rebecca Tharrington*

Marjorie Harris Carr Cross Florida Greenway. Long name and a long greenway. Length is one of the good things about greenways. They typically stretch many miles throughout the state, linking vital ecological and cultural resources, forests, recreational trailheads, etc. This one runs from the Gulf near Yankeetown to the Rodman Reservoir, almost to Palatka. Greenways are shared by humans and animals alike. Actually, the trail bridge crossing over I-75 in the west was designed to accommodate animals as well as other user groups. Unpaved and adorned with only Florida native plant species, it's well worth a side trip. Moreover, the singletrack leading to it from CR-475A is a blast to ride.

Out of the negative came the positive. The entire greenway property resulted from an ill-fated, controversial, ecologically doomed project called the Cross Florida Barge Canal. Thankfully, it never came to fruition and was officially terminated in the late 1960's. See the Cross Florida Greenway writeup in the Honorable Mention section for a detailed account of this property.

Trail Map Legend below (trail names & features): 1. Dog Bone 2. Jungle 3. Bus Stop 4. Twister 4a. Short Leg 5. Brass Ring 6. Vortex 7. Bike Shop 8. Bill's Wicked Trail 9. Baby Head 10. ICU 11. Marshmallow 12. Sinkhole 12a. Dr. Ruth's Run 13. Pine Tree 14. Irish's Trail 15. Canopy 16. Maclane's Trail 17. Rattlesnake 18. Ant Hill 19. John Brown 20. Snake 21. Magic Mountain 22. Bunny 23. Termite.

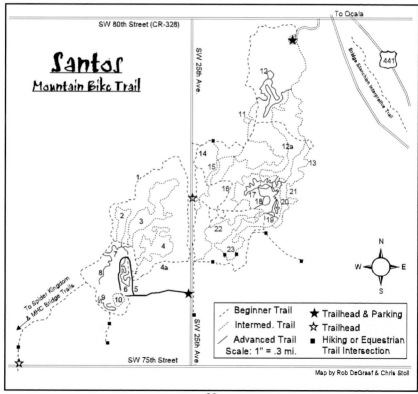

Most call it Santos, some call it Belleview, others call it the Cross Florida Barge Canal, but everyone calls it awesome. Santos is the name of the small town where the main trailhead is located. Belleview, while bigger, is further south. It appears on more maps than Santos. A standardized trail marking system is used here: beginner trails are marked in yellow and have little technical difficulty; intermediate trails are blue and have increased technical difficulty; finally, advanced trails are red and provide steep climbs and descents, tight turns, and a significant increase of technical terrain. Most of the red trails are in and around old borrow pits. Trails are all one way with up arrows indicating the trail is straight ahead while a down arrow means "Don't enter." Trail surfaces range from sand and loam in the wooded areas to rock and clay in the borrow pits.

The extensive, spider's web-like network of trails makes it very easy for the new arrival to get lost. There are so many trail choices. Take one look at the map and you'll get a good idea of the navigation you're up against. Luckily, locals and regu-

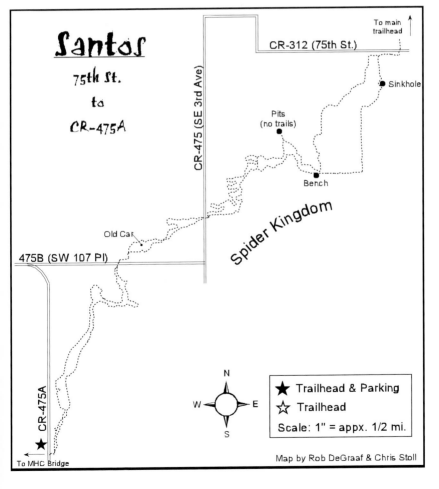

lars are always willing to direct you back to your vehicle. However, don't rely on someone else to help you find your way back. On weekdays or in certain regions of the trail, help may be a long way off. Take responsibility for your ride and plan ahead. Bring a compass. They're small and light thus should be included as standard ride gear. Maps are usually available at the main trailhead or use those provided here. The loop out through Spider Kingdom heads far west over the land bridge crossing I-75 and exceeds 20 miles. OMBA has not only built beautiful rhythm into these trails but they have intentionally run the trails down old fence lines enshrouded by huge oak trees. This makes for a cooler ride and the fallen leaves mix with the soil to preserve an enduring trail surface.

Wildlife: Most species are more common further west within the Greenway. Whitetail deer, rabbit, feral hog, armadillo, raccoon, opossum, turkey, endangered gopher tortoise, eastern diamond-back rattlesnake, hawk, vulture, owls, occasional sandhill crane in open prairie sections, and many more. Trees & plants include live oak, scrub oak, slash, sand and long leaf pine, magnolia, cabbage palm, saw palmetto, boston fern, resurrection fern, beautyberry, lantana, etc.

Et cetera: Size: 81,290 acres (entire greenway). Marion County. Helmets required. Bring plenty of food and water (several bottles and/ or a hydration pack). A map and compass are recommended as is a first-aid kit; know how to use each. Also bring a couple of spare tubes, a pump and any vital tools. This is a wild area encompassing thousands of acres so you want to be prepared. I've run into new riders here many times who were hopelessly lost, very worn out, and very far from their vehicles. Plan ahead! There is potable water and restrooms at the main trailhead. Other activities include hiking, nature study and horseback riding. Be on the lookout for hiking and horseback rider trail intersections, and be courteous by yielding trail to these users at that time!

When to Go: Fall, winter, and spring are the most enjoyable seasons to bike here, as they are cooler and drier. Trails are typically fast drying even after summer downpours.

Contacts: Ocala Mountain Bike Association, on the web at: www.omba.org or contact the Florida Department of Environmental Protection, Office of Greenways and Trails, Ocala Office: (352) 236-7143.

Directions: Several trailheads exist. Main one is located in Santos. From I-75: take exit #341 (CR-484). Head east appx. 2 miles to traffic light at CR-475. Make left heading north. Continue north for appx. 5 miles to traffic light at 80th St. Turn right and proceed east 3 miles to the trailhead on your right just before reaching US-301/ 441. From Ocala at SR-40: head south on US-301/ 441 for appx. 6 miles. Just after 301 splits, turn right onto 80th Street (CR-328) and look for entrance on your left . . . The trail crosses several paved roads. Of these, only a couple have ample parking and have no restrooms or potable water. These are (from east to west): CR-475A; from I-75 take exit #341 (CR-484). Head east appx. 1/4 mile to first major left onto CR-475A. Head north a couple miles watching for trailhead on your left. This is the best place to access the MHC Land Bridge over I-75 and the best place to begin rides of Santos' western trails . . . 49th Ave; from I-75 take exit #341 (CR-484). Head west appx. 2 ½ miles to a right on 49th Ave. Follow 49th north as it curves to left then branches off again to the right heading due north. Watch for trailhead on your right. Once on your bike, ride north along a shared use trail, paralleling 49th Ave. Look for the yellow OMBA trailhead near the western base of an old sand pit/ hill. Note: at time of writing, the trail from here was still being developed, thus, contact OMBA before heading to this trailhead as there may (or may not be) any worthwhile riding here yet. OMBA informed us that this trail segment was halfway done.

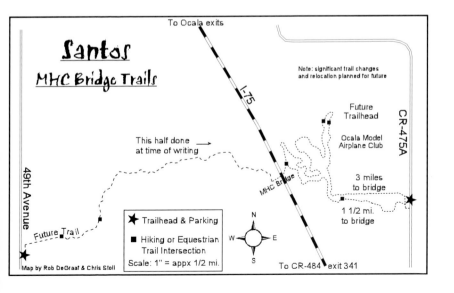

Ocala National Forest - Paisley Woods

Location: Within Ocala National Forest. Deland is closest town.

Managing Agency: U.S. Department of Agriculture, Forest Service Southern Region.

Trail Length: 22 miles.

Difficulty: 20% beginner; 80% intermediate.

Trail Type: 100% singletrack.

Description: The Paisley Woods Bicycle Trail winds through a scenic longleaf pine-wiregrass ecosystem. The trail, constructed specifically for bicyclists, was finished in 1995. It was developed by the Lake County Bicycle and Pedestrian Program, Lake County Rails to Trails and the Florida Freewheelers in cooperation with the Ocala National Forest. The trail's gentle, sweeping curves wind through moderately undulating hills as it transverses live oak domes, grassy prairies and stands of pine of varying ages. If you seek solitude you've come to the right place. Unlike Ocala's other premier trails, Paisley Woods is very lightly visited. This in part is due to its remoteness. Ocala is around 30 to 45 minutes away, and Deland, while much smaller, is 15 to 20 minutes east of here. Also, Paisley Woods is very different from the more technical, roller-coaster like rock quarry trails around Ocala. Paisley is a place to head when you desire, foremost, increased solitude and heightened wildlife viewing opportunities. While accomplishing these goals you can at the same time log some serious mileage.

The entire 22-mile singletrack loop takes an average biker 6 to 8 hours, however, shorter ride options exist. The trail is shaped like a figure-8, with two distinct loops (north and south) and a short (.3 mi.) connector trail midway (see map). This design was created so riders could do shorter loops, in the north or the south, 11.1 miles and 10 miles respectively. The trail is marked with yellow diamonds and posts at intersections and road crossings. Care must be taken to look for these diamonds following every road crossing as false trails, for motorcycles or equestrians, can be taken accidently. If you do not see the yellow diamonds immediately after a crossing, you probably have missed the trail.

Alexander Springs Recreation Area is located on the north end of the trail and Clearwater Lake Recreation Area is on the south. Water, flush toilets and showers are available at both sites with a concession at Alexander Springs. Both areas charge an entrance fee, however, the safety of parking your vehicle there, coupled with the availability of being able to take a swim at the end of your ride, makes the fee nominal. Free parking with NO facilities is available on FR-538 half a mile southeast from CR-445. This trailhead is so close to Alexander Springs (.9 mi.) however that it makes more sense to park at the latter.

Plant and animal life is protected in the Forest. For your safety, do not attempt to pet, feed or approach wildlife and be wary of poisonous snakes and plants. Eastern dia

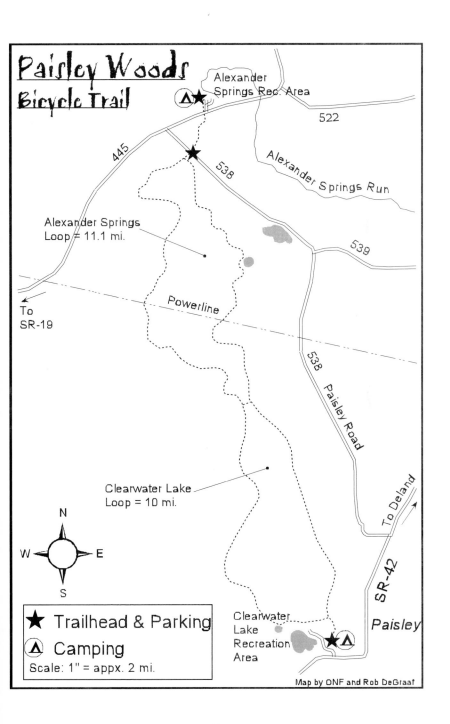

Paisley Woods
Bicycle Trail

Alexander
Springs Rec. Area

522

445

538

Alexander Springs Run

Alexander Springs
Loop = 11.1 mi.

539

Powerline

To
SR-19

538 Paisley Road

To Deland

Clearwater Lake
Loop = 10 mi.

N

W — E

S

SR-42

Clearwater
Lake
Recreation
Area

Paisley

★ Trailhead & Parking

Ⓐ Camping

Scale: 1" = appx. 2 mi.

Map by ONF and Rob DeGraaf

33

mondback rattle snakes make habitat in the forest's dry upland terrain. At time of writing, unauthorized trail use by ATVs on the south end of the trail had widened and softened it. Other portions of the trail can become soft, especially during prolonged dry weather. A rule to remember is: sand is better as it gets wetter. Thus, riding especially soft sections is much more enjoyable after a rain.

<u>Wildlife:</u> The Forest is prime habitat to many sensitive, rare and endangered species and ecosystems. Black bear and gopher tortoise are found here. Whitetail deer are common. Depending on when you ride, viewing certain species can be challenging as most are reclusive, making their way out of hiding typically during dawn or dusk hours. Deer are somewhat common. Florida black bear, on the endangered species list, are pretty well established in Ocala National Forest, perhaps more so than anywhere else within the state. However, extreme luck, timing and silence are still key ingredients for getting to see bear here. Most flatwoods ecosystems in Florida are comprised of slash pine/ palmetto. Here, however, the visitor is presented with the somewhat less common, longleaf pine-wiregrass community. . . . birds of prey (e.g., red-shouldered hawk, barred owl, etc.) outnumber wading birds here due to lack of appropriate habitat for latter.

<u>Et cetera:</u> Ocala NF size: 383,573 acres. Lake County. Helmets required. Fee assessed if entering either Alexander Springs or Clearwater Lake Recreation Areas. At time of writing, trail maintenance seemed slack but perhaps things will improve by press time. Remember, water is not available along the trail so stock up before heading out. Potable water can be found at either recreation area at both major trailheads listed above and shown on map. Many other fun recreational opportunities can be found in the National Forest (of course, none equal off-road bicycling!): hiking on the Florida National Scenic Trail (with trail sections adjacent to Paisley Woods Bicycle Trail at CR-538 trailhead), hiking too many other trails to name, paddling several rivers and spring runs (e.g., Alexander Springs, Juniper, etc.), swimming, snorkeling or SCUBA diving in too many springs to name, camping (both primitive and with facilities), horseback riding, fishing, nature study, picnicking, and just plain old exploring the forest. It's a vast, wonderful place and some of the acreage is federally designated wilderness area.

<u>When to Go:</u> There is adequate shade for summer morning or evening riding but the sandy sections will be more firm after rain. Winter riding may be cooler but it is also much drier meaning that more sugar sand may be encountered. Also, call for hunt dates before heading out (typically during winter months). In spite of the great shape you are in, you are undoubtedly slower than a speeding bullet. While most hunters identify their targets before shooting, a few may show less restraint and some may object to you spooking animals.

<u>Contacts:</u> Seminole Ranger District, Ocala National Forest, 40929 State Road 19, Umatilla, FL 32784, (352) 669-3153; Pittman Visitor Center, 45621 State Road 19, Altoona, FL 32702, (352) 669-7495.

Directions: To northern trailheads, from Ocala: head east on SR-40, entering the National Forest and passing SR-19. Turn right onto FR-445 heading south. 445 will make a sharp bend to the right. Alexander Springs will be less than a mile on your right, and the northern trailhead will be directly across 445 from the Alexander Springs entrance. Best to park inside the Recreation Area for vehicle security and proximity to amenities like restrooms, water, swimming, etc . . . Alternate trailhead (with no facilities) just west of Alexander Springs on FR-538 (Paisley Rd.). The trail actually crosses 538 here so it's easy to find. . . From the south, at intersection of SR-42 and SR-19 in Altoona, head north to FR-445. Make a right heading appx. 5 miles to trailheads described above . . . To southern trailhead: from junction of SR-42 and SR-19 in Altoona, head east on 42 for appx. 6.5 miles to the entrance of Clearwater Lake Recreation Area on the left. Park immediately to your right in the paved parking area and look for the trail heading north from here . . . From points east, follow SR-42 west. 42 will bend due south then head due west in Johnson's Corner. Clearwater Rec. Area entrance will be appx. 1 mile west of this bend.

Withlacoochee State Forest - Croom Tract

Location: Northeast of Brooksville.

Managing Agency: Florida Division of Forestry

Trail Length: Appx. 50 miles.

Difficulty: 60% Beginner, 35% Intermediate, 5% Advanced

Trail Type: 100% singletrack

Description: This is a great place to see deer if you ride quietly. Croom is a large tract of land comprised of longleaf and slash pine, scrub and turkey oak, hardwood hammocks, cypress ponds and creek bottoms most of which offer deer a place to hide. Beginning in 1890, the lands within Croom were used for phosphate mining. It soon became one of the country's largest such mines, with huge shipments of rock frequently being sent to Belgium, Germany and other regions around the globe. Old tram roads, used to facilitate the removal of phosphate, still crisscross the landscape, affording the cyclist with "historic" elevation changes! Winding trails were originally created by motorcyclists during an annual race event. The motorcycle races continue to this day, and oftentimes remaining trail is inherited and used as new bike trails. The SWAMP Club of Tampa spent years advocating for permission to mark and maintain these trails for mountain bikers. Some of the trail was rerouted to better suit the needs of mountain bikers but the creation of the fun whoop-te-doos is a debt we owe the motorcyclists.

While Rudy is a seasoned veteran of Croom's terrain, Rob's first trip here was in 1994. Rob writes: on a solo mission one short winter day I headed out from the Tucker Hill trailhead. Lacking a trail map, compass, or local trail knowledge, I soon realized that I had taken a wrong turn somewhere. What the correct route was and how much trail remained was unclear. With two hours of remaining sunlight, a race against time ensued. My (one) water bottle contained a dwindling twenty ounces. Lying ahead, thirty to forty miles of sinuous trail stretched through darkening, endless pine woods. Visibility waned. While the trail was incredible, it was unexpectedly long. I pedaled on, and on, and on. Just as conditions really became dark, a faint, white glint of dirt road was spotted in the distance. I had finally reached Croom Road, exhausted and relieved! This particular ride taught me a big lesson: always plan ahead and ride prepared. On large properties like Croom, bringing extra gear "just in case" is always a wise idea. Watch for inconspicuous forks or trail intersections. Lastly, if unfamiliar with a certain trail, ride with a local.

Wildlife: Whitetail deer, feral hog, armadillo, rabbit, coyote, bobcat, raccoon, opossum, turkey, endangered gopher tortoise, indigo snake, eastern diamond-back rattlesnake, red-shouldered hawk, red fox, etc. Plant communities include slash, sand and long leaf pine, turkey oak, sand live oak, palmetto, gallberry, sparkleberry, beautyberry, to name just a few. Ask the State Forest for a complete list.

Et cetera: Size: 21,639 acres. Hernando County. Helmets required. Potable water is available at the parking area at Tucker Hill (Trailhead #3). Kiosk at trailhead. Bring plenty of food and water (several bottles and/ or a hydration pack). A map and compass are recommended as is a first-aid kit; know how to use each. Also bring a couple of spare tubes, a pump, any vital tools, a lightweight rain-coat, and insect repellent. This is a wild area encompassing thousands of acres. Prescribed burns in sections. If you ride, you need to help maintain your trails. Contact SWAMP for trail work dates. Section of the Florida Trail (for hiking only) crosses the property. Caution: riding in "The Pits" can be thrilling but it is where most of the personal injuries and bicycle carnage take place so be especially careful if you are not experienced.

When to Go: While Croom is certainly enjoyable any time of year, it is one of the few Central Florida places that are great to ride in the summer. Summer rains tend to pack the sandy soil sections of the trail into a hard, smooth, very fast surface. Shade from the trees diminishes the effects of the hot sun. Once your shirt gets damp it is not too hot if you keep a good pace. Check the hunting schedule late October through December and don't ride when hunting is allowed. In spite of the great shape you are in, you are undoubtedly slower than a speeding bullet. While most hunters identify their targets before shooting, a few may show less restraint and some may object to you spooking animals.

Contacts: Withlacoochee State Forest Recreation Center, 15003 Broad St., Brooksville, FL 34601, (352) 754-6896. On the web: www.fl-dof.com; SWAMP Club: 9401 Takomah Trail, Tampa, FL 33617 (813) 985-5021. www.swampclub.org

Directions: From I-75 take exit #301, State Road 50. Head one mile east on SR-50 then turn left onto Croom Rital Road. Head north appx. 5 miles. Eastern parking (Trailhead #1) is on both sides of Croom Rital Rd. where it crosses the Withlacoochee State Trail the second time. Other parking areas and trailheads are further west from here. Croom Rital Road bends to the left, heading west, and becomes the gravel Croom Rd. Trailhead #2 is located appx. 2.5 miles west at the intersection of Forest Road #7 and Croom Rd. The bike trail heads north and south from here on the west side of FR#7. Another 3 miles west leads to Trailhead #3 at Tucker Hill. This is the main trailhead. Potable water and ranger headquarters are located here.

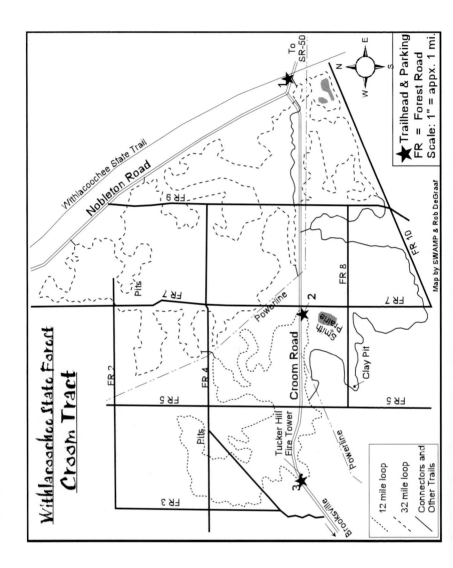

Withlacoochee State Forest
Croom Tract

★ Trailhead & Parking
FR = Forest Road
Scale: 1" = appx. 1 mi.

Map by SWAMP & Rob DeGraaf

Withlacoochee State Trail

Nobleton Road

To SR-50

FR 9

FR 10

Pits

FR 7

FR 8

Powerline

Smith Prairie

Clay Pit

FR 2

FR 4

FR 5

FR 7

Croom Road

Tucker Hill Fire Tower

Powerline

Pits

FR 3

FR 5

Brooksville

1

2

3

······ 12 mile loop
- - - 32 mile loop
——— Connectors and Other Trails

Lower Hillsborough Wilderness Park

Location: Tampa: Morris Bridge Park, Trout Creek Park and Flatwoods Park

Managing Agency: Hillsborough County Parks and Recreation Department

Trail Length: Approximately 35 miles total; main loop trail is 18 miles

Difficulty: 80% beginner; 20% intermediate

Trail Type: 90% singletrack; 8% doubletrack; 2% pavement

Description: The thick, native woods beckon to you and your trail-eager steed, compelling you to enter, explore, and enjoy the many miles of sweet off-road trail lying within. Once cruising down the trail, your wheels will encounter mostly flat, semi-fast, often rooty, hardpack singletrack. Wilderness Park trails are conspicuously consistent, allowing one an excellent aerobic workout with very few sudden stops. Variations that you will find are mostly aesthetic: for instance, crossing from dry, upland sections, into lower lying cypress edged swamps. Flatwoods and Trout Creek Parks have much of the former, while Morris Bridge has much of the latter. Moreover, most of the lower lying trails are prone to flooding from nearby Cow House Slough, thus are "seasonal." These trails also house some of the best technical sections in that they are increasingly rooty, slick after rains, and often festooned with downed logs. "Indian," "Misery," and "Gator Bait" are prime examples of flat, technical, root strewn trails.

Wilderness Park is comprised of three tracts: Morris Bridge, Trout Creek, and Flatwoods. An 18 mile long, mostly off-road trail connects the three. This "main loop trail" was christened in July 1998, and came as the result of multi-party efforts including: Wilderness Trails Association (WTA), the SWAMP club, SWFWMD, and Hillsborough County Parks and Recreation. Within the park, there is a 16,000 acre "flood detention area" owned by SWFWMD. Part of this tract is managed by the county for recreation. . . . The loop trail is marked with numbered, wooden posts. Match the post numbers to those on the trail map to find your location. The main trail can be accessed at five different locations (directions for each listed below): Morris Bridge, Hole-in-the-Fence, Trout Creek Park, Flatwoods Park and Bruce B. Downs Blvd.

In general, the loop trail affords the easiest off-road riding in Wilderness Park. It is comprised of mostly singletrack, some doubletrack, some off-road levee, some paved and shared-use sections in Flatwoods Park, and a short stretch of Morris Bridge Road as it crosses the scenic Hillsborough River. The loop trail crosses Morris Bridge Road a second time as it connects Morris Bridge to Trout Creek Park. Morris Bridge Road is shared by vehicles, so use extreme caution when crossing or riding along the road.

Morris Bridge, compared to the other sites, has many creatively named trails to choose from (see map). Having a trail map is very helpful here, especially for the uninitiated. First timers may also want to bring a compass.

The "Pits" section is most quickly accessed by biking in from the Hole-in-the-

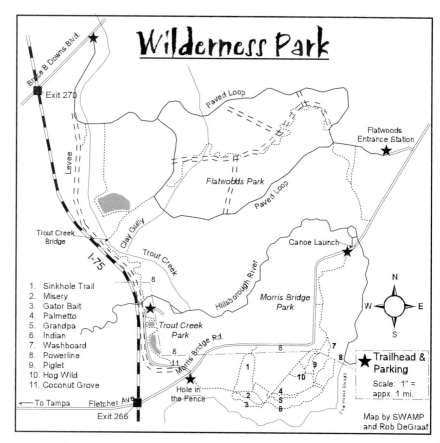

Wilderness Park

Bruce B Downs Blvd.

Exit 270

Paved Loop

Flatwoods Entrance Station

Levee

Flatwoods Park

Paved Loop

Clay Gully

Trout Creek Bridge

Trout Creek

Hillsborough River

Canoe Launch

I-75

Morris Bridge Park

1. Sinkhole Trail
2. Misery
3. Gator Bait
4. Palmetto
5. Grandpa
6. Indian
7. Washboard
8. Powerline
9. Piglet
10. Hog Wild
11. Coconut Grove

Trout Creek Park

Morris Bridge Rd.

Hole in the Fence

← To Tampa   Fletcher Ave.

Exit 266

N
W — E
S

★ Trailhead & Parking

Scale: 1" = appx. 1 mi.

Map by SWAMP and Rob DeGraaf

Fence trailhead. Many different, short trails span this small, low lying ravine-like section. Use caution when approaching as the sand is soft, unstable and unpredictable. Injuries have occurred here.

Much of the singletrack trail through Flatwoods Park crisscrosses, and sometimes shares company with, a doubletrack road. If need be, this road can serve as a faster route out of the park (in either direction), and eventually will lead one to the seven mile paved, shared-use trail. There is an interesting, historic cabin to explore off of the "Cabin Trail" in Flatwoods Park.

Trout Creek Park has the shortest trail mileage of the three sites, however, it also has one of the most gnarly, palmetto-root sections of trail along the entire loop (in southern section). The trail parallels the shores of several nice lakes providing decent fishing and bird-watching opportunities. The flood control structure is located in Trout Creek Park. Its gates close ½ hour before park closes, so watch your watch!

<u>Wildlife:</u> Whitetail deer, feral hog, armadillo, raccoon, opossum, turkey, endangered gopher tortoise, eastern diamond-back rattlesnake, cottonmouth, yellow-rat snake, alligator, river otter, limpkin, ibis, egrets, herons, roseate spoonbill, myriad dragonflies and damselflies, etc. Trees & plants include live oak, scrub oak, bald

cypress, slash pine, magnolia, cabbage palm, saw palmetto, boston fern, resurrection fern, string fern, etc.

Et cetera: Size: over 7,200 acres. Hillsborough County. Call for current hours. Gates atop flood control structure close ½ hour before the park closes. Bring plenty of food and water (several bottles and/ or a hydration pack). A map and compass are recommended as is a first-aid kit; know how to use each. Also bring a couple of spare tubes, a pump, any vital tools, a lightweight rain-coat, and insect repellent. This is a wild area encompassing thousands of acres.

Restrooms at Morris Bridge (canoe launch), Trout Creek and Flatwoods trailheads. Water at bathrooms. "Ice cold" water along paved loop in Flatwoods. Bike wash available at Trout Creek and Flatwoods. Payphones at Flatwoods, Morris Bridge, and Trout Creek. Minimal amenities at Hole-in-the-Fence and Bruce B. Downs trailheads. Trail maps usually available at each site. $1 "honor pay" entrance fee at Trout Creek, Hole-in-the-Fence, Flatwoods, and the Bruce B. Downs entrance. Flatwoods Park boasts an additional seven mile paved, shared use, trail. Note: off-road trails shared with hikers, runners and dog-walkers. Other recreational opportunities include: hiking on trails and boardwalks, canoeing/ kayaking, fishing, nature study, and horseback riding. The Hillsborough river is incredibly scenic and is a highly suggested paddle trip!

The Wilderness Trails Association (WTA) meets for trail work at 9am on 3rd Saturday of each month at the Morris Bridge Canoe Launch area (where Morris Bridge Road crosses Hillsborough River). Come lend a hand. WTA also has monthly meetings on 1st Wednesday of each month at Flatwoods Park Entrance Station. WTA membership is free. Trail steward program also. Contact SWAMP to ask about winter, weekly night rides.

When to Go: Fall, winter, and spring are the most enjoyable seasons to bike here, as they are cooler and much drier. Certain Morris Bridge trails are seasonal, in that they are often closed during summer wet months or after pervasive rains. Conversely, prolonged dry weather can create soft and sandy conditions on many Morris Bridge trails, especially in the pits area.

Contacts: Hillsborough County Parks and Recreation Department, 1101 E. River Cove, Tampa, FL 33604, (813) 975-2160; Wilderness Park: (813) 987-6211; Wilderness Trails Association (WTA): ask SWAMP for current contact info; SWAMP Club: 9401 Takomah Trail, Tampa, FL 33617, (813) 985-5021. www.swampclub.org

Directions: *To Morris Bridge* "Hole in the Fence:" From I-75. Fletcher Avenue east, becomes Morris Bridge Road. Turn right into first dirt road immediately after road curves to the left; . . . *Morris Bridge Canoe Launch*: From I-75. Fletcher Avenue east, becomes Morris Bridge Road. Follow Morris Bridge Road several miles, then make a left into parking area just before crossing the Hillsborough River; . . . *Trout Creek trailhead*: From I-75. Fletcher Avenue east, becomes Morris Bridge Road. Turn left into first paved road. Look for Trout Creek Park sign. Follow paved road into parking area. Bike south back down paved road and look for trailhead on east side of paved road; . . . *Flatwoods Park trailhead*: From I-75. Fletcher Avenue east, becomes Morris Bridge Road. Follow Morris Bridge Road north as it crosses the Hillsborough River. Turn left into Flatwoods Park a couple miles after crossing the river. Park at "entrance station" about a ½ mile on right. Bike along the paved loop and enter off-road trail at various locations; . . *Bruce B. Downs Blvd*: from Tampa, follow Bruce B. Downs Blvd. (CR-581) north, past I-75, several miles. Trailhead and parking area are on right (east), just after Home Depot. A paved trail from here leads to access for the off-road, main loop trail. Make your first right at the levee to head into Trout Creek Park, OR cross Trout Creek then make a right onto marked doubletrack trail to head into Flatwoods Park (see map).

Trout Creek Bridge

Photo by Rebecca Tharrington

Carter Road Park

★ Trailhead & Parking
▲ Bridge
∴ Singletrack
═ Dirt Roads

Scale: 1" = appx. 900'

Soccer Field
Baseball Diamonds
Main Park Road
Residence
Doubletrack
Sprinkler Hill
Sand Pit
Open Field
Snake Ridge
Puff n Stuff
Sneaky Snake
Horseshoe Ridge
The Beast
Gate
The Green Mile
Note: ridges in this area are extremely technical and are optional. Experts only.
Stinky Finger
Optional
Climb
Roller Coaster

Map by
Rob DeGraaf & Kent Hickman

43

Carter Road Park

Location: Between Lakeland and Mulberry

Managing Agency: Polk County Parks and Recreation Department

Trail Length: 6.2 miles

Difficulty: 30% beginner; 50% intermediate; 20% advanced

Trail Type: 90% singletrack; 10% dirt roads

Description: First and foremost, a huge thanks needs to be given to the Lakeland based Ridge Riders Mountain-Bike Association (RRMBA). RRMBA advocated for off-road bicycle trails here in 1996, and since then have provided constant nurturing and grooming to the trails making them some of central Florida's best. Still, Carter is a work in progress. New trails continue to be designed as time passes, adding new mileage and new challenges. Credit also needs to go to Polk County, who has been very receptive to trail development here over the years.

This property was used for phosphate mining in the '40s and '50s. Phosphate mining is certainly still one of the largest business activities in Polk County. Typically, areas are mined over many years. Then, when resources are depleted, the sites are usually environmentally reclaimed and reused for other purposes. Dirt (usually clay and gypsum) mounds and ridges, known as "tailings," are remnants of mining activity. Over many years, nature recovers on and around the tailings creating vegetation on the hilly terrain. Carter's awesome topography is a prime example of past mining activity turned mountain-biking venue.

The park is best known for its roller-coaster like, narrow, smooth, hardpack ridge trails. The ridges have many climbs and descents, some of which are quite steep. Roots and rocks, while not very common, can appear unexpectedly, so caution is advised. Balance and momentum are crucial when riding atop the ridges. A fall here can be nasty, as many of the ridges are as high as thirty or more feet. Murky green water waits below.

Fortunately, novice riders are not forced to ride the technical sections. Each difficult trail section can easily be bypassed via adjacent trails and dirt roads, all of which are easy to find. In fact, an enjoyable loop of dirt roads and novice singletrack trails can be completed rather easily by following the map.

A few of the main sections are: Sprinkler Hill; shady (huge oaks), sinuous, well bermed, hilly hardpack, leading into Horseshoe Ridge; intermediate level hardpack ridge, undulating, shady, smooth, makes a U-turn. And, The Beast; advanced level section, scrappy, technical climbs and descents, littered with roots and rocks, you'll want to turn around and ride it again.

Wildlife: Armadillo, raccoon, opossum, bobcat, alligator, various snakes, grey squirrel, wading birds, etc. One evening I saw four rabbits adjacent to the sidewalk and paved road near trailhead. Flora consists of oak, slash pine, Brazilian pepper, willow, Boston fern, muscadine grape, lantana, gallberry, beautyberry, caesar's weed, poke weed, smilax, etc.

Et cetera: Size: 400+ acres. Polk County. Hours: 7:00 am to sunset. Helmets required. Restrooms in park. Bring plenty of food and water (several bottles and/ or a hydration pack), first-aid kit and sun-screen if desired. Also bring a couple of spare tubes, a pump and vital tools. Use trail map in Guide or obtain one at trailhead. No park entrance fee. Kiosk at trailhead. Bike wash between soccer fields. Most ride directional loop beginning with Sprinkler Hill section. Following this advice will save potential head-on crashes as well as sideways glances and comments from locals! Other common park activities include fishing (by land and boat), baseball and soccer. Lots of food and services north from park on SR-37 (Florida Ave.), including Mexican at Tres Pesos on west side of 37 just south of the Polk Pkwy. Call RRMBA to inquire about trail work days. If you ride, you need to help maintain your trails. Races are held from fall through spring.

When to Go: Fall, winter, and spring are the most enjoyable seasons to bike here, as they are cooler and much drier, however, trail drains quickly after summer rains. Much of the trail is clay, thus can become slick after rainfall.

Contacts: Polk County Parks and Recreation Department: (863) 534-4340; Ridge-Riders Mountain-bike Club: (863) 619-5001. Website: www.ridgeriders.net

Directions: From Lakeland (at US-92), head south appx. 9 miles on SR-37 (Florida Ave.). Make left heading east on Carter Road. Drive a short distance before making a right into park. Follow paved road as it curves 90 degrees to left. Continue straight ahead to mountain-bike parking area. . . . From the south, Mulberry at SR-60: take SR-37 (Florida Ave.) north appx. 2 ½ miles. Make right heading east on Carter Road, then follow directions above.

Photo by Rebecca Tharrington

Rob negotiates a climb at Carter Park

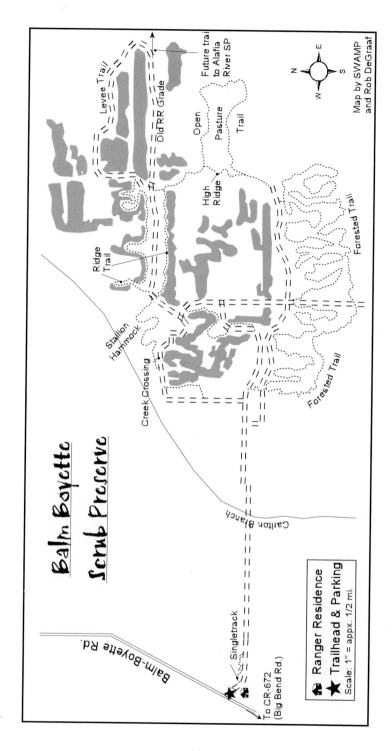

Balm Boyette Scrub Preserve

Levee Trail

Old RR Grade

Future trail to Alafia River SP

Open Pasture Trail

High Ridge

Ridge Trail

Stallion Hammock

Creek Crossing

Forested Trail

Forested Trail

Carlton Branch

Singletrack

Balm-Boyette Rd.

To CR-672 (Big Bend Rd.)

N
W   E
S

Map by SWAMP and Rob DeGraaf

🏠 Ranger Residence
⭐ Trailhead & Parking

Scale: 1" = appx. 1/2 mi.

46

Balm Boyette Scrub Preserve

Location: Nearest towns: Wimauma and Riverview

Managing Agency: Hillsborough County Parks and Recreation Department

Trail Length: 18 miles

Difficulty: 35% beginner; 60% intermediate; 5% advanced

Trail Type: 70% singletrack; 30% doubletrack

Description: A tunnel of green rushes past as your eyes lead your bike into one turn after the next. Hundreds of well designed twists and turns more than make up for the lack of appreciable elevation change. Boyette's trails seem to have an almost unexplainable, inherent "flow" that is really fun to experience. Be prepared to enter a Zen-like state of awareness as you steer through scenic and native scrub oak, slash and sand pine, and saw palmetto. Most of the trail mileage is sinuous, fast, flat, hardpack singletrack mixed with a smattering of palmetto roots (a.k.a., gator-backs), other roots and the occasional log. Sand, while never a big problem, can form in sections during very dry weather.

What's interesting about Boyette is its diversity of terrain: miles of woodsy singletrack combine with open, semi-technical ridge trails bordering picturesque lakes. The lakes are the remnants of once active phosphate mines. There is also a ravine-like section in open prairie (eastern section of property) where the trail snakes its way back and forth, up and down, and side to side, the shallow ravine. The adjacent ridge affords an excellent, expansive view of the surrounding terrain. You may not feel like you're in Florida out here. For those who like to defy gravity, there are several decent jumps in this section. However, I suggest you scout the trail prior to making like a bird and taking flight!

Planned for the near future: be sure to check out the linkage trail connecting Boyette with its eastern neighbor, Alafia River State Park (see map for trail location and see Guide for Alafia). The trail makes use of a long abandoned railway corridor and provides a connection to even more adjacent trail mileage. The Tampa based SWAMP Club has done an incredible job of creating and maintaining these trails for our off-road bicycling pleasure. If you come across any local SWAMP'ers, be sure to thank them for their efforts!

Wildlife: Whitetail deer, feral hog, armadillo, rabbit, raccoon, opossum, turkey, endangered gopher tortoise, indigo snake, eastern diamond-back rattlesnake, scrub jay, red-shouldered hawk, red fox, swallowtail butterfly, rare Florida golden aster, and more. Rumor has it that two riders have seen what "looked like" a Florida Panther on the property.

Et cetera: Size: 4,916 acres. Hillsborough County. Hours: sunrise to sunset. Helmets required. No entrance fee. There is only one main route into the heart of

Boyette: this is by following the two-mile, east-west doubletrack road. An often sandy section of this doubletrack can be bypassed via a short singletrack trail on north side of road.

Security resident lives near trailhead. Maps and kiosk at trailhead. Bring plenty of food and water (several bottles and/ or a hydration pack). A map and compass are recommended as is a first-aid kit; know how to use each. Also bring a couple of spare tubes, a pump, any vital tools, a lightweight rain-coat, and insect repellent. This is a wild area encompassing thousands of acres. Prescribed burns in sections. Call the county for most recent information. If you ride, you need to help maintain your trails. Contact SWAMP for trail work dates. Excellent hiking potential in section of preserve on west side of Balm-Boyette Road. Good fishing opportunities in Boyette's many lakes. Local food choices: Mexican in Wimauma and Burke & Howie's in Riverview.

When to Go: Fall, winter, and spring are the most enjoyable seasons to bike here, as they are cooler and much drier. There is little to no shade in the open prairie sections making them extremely hot and humid in the summer. Keep hydrated and conserve your energy. Trail conditions are usually decent throughout the year, although with extremes of dryness or wetness, sandy sections or flooded/ muddy sections, respectively, can form.

Contacts: Hillsborough County Parks and Recreation Department: (813) 975-2160; SWAMP Club: 9401 Takomah Trail, Tampa, FL 33617, (813) 985-5021. www.swampclub.org

Directions: From I-75: From the north; take CR-672 (Big Bend Rd.) exit. Head east approximately 4 miles then turn right on Balm Road. Stay on Balm for about 3 ½ miles, as it curves to the left. Make left on Balm-Wimauma Road and head north 1 mile. Trailhead is on right at small dirt parking area. . . From the south; take CR-674 exit. Head east 6 ½ miles through town of Wimauma. Make left, heading north, onto Balm-Boyette Road. Road bends to the right after around 3 miles, then bears left as it crosses CR-672. Trailhead is 1 mile north of CR-672 at small dirt parking area on right.

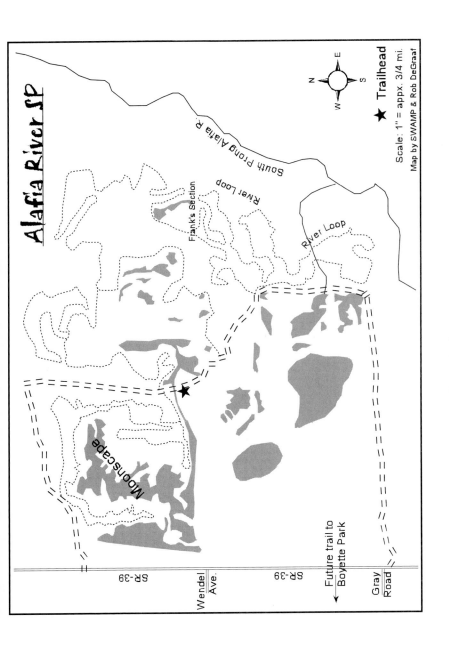

Alafia River SP

Frank's Section

River Loop

River Loop

South Prong Alafia R.

Moonscape

SR-39

Wendel Ave.

SR-39

Future trail to Boyette Park

Gray Road

★ Trailhead

Scale: 1" = appx. 3/4 mi.

Map by SWAMP & Rob DeGraaf

Alafia River State Park

Location: In Lithia. Wimauma and Riverview nearby

Managing Agency: Florida Department of Environmental Protection, Division of Recreation and Parks

Trail Length: 14 miles (20 - 25 planned)

Difficulty: 10% beginner; 50% intermediate; 40% advanced

Trail Type: 95% singletrack; 5% doubletrack

Description: When a mountain bike trail earns Olympic recognition, you can bet your you know what that the trails at such a place were painstakingly, skillfully crafted over several years of hard work. If Tampa would have been selected to host the 2012 Olympic Games, Alafia, it was predetermined, would have been the venue for the mountain bike competition. The only bad news is that Tampa lost out on this bid. Good news is that this didn't affect the trails in any way, shape or form.

In September 2000, Tampa's SWAMP Club was given permission to begin flagging new trail on the Alafia property. At that time, the park was a State Recreation Area (SRA), however, very minimal recreation actually took place here, excepting light equestrian, hiking and fishing use. Things progressed slowly regarding trail development and a waiting game ensued. SWAMP had to wait for the park to get its re-designation plans in order and to construct new internal roads, main entrances, campgrounds, new facilities, etc. This wait gave plenty of time for volunteers to patiently scout and mark new trails to be constructed. Creating great trails in any terrain takes time. Factoring in significant elevation change (in old phosphate areas) only adds to the needed planning and cooperative trail work. In a few sections, the IMBA Trail Care Crew was recruited to lend their expertise. The result was several rerouted climbs and bench cuts. Very few, if any, trails in Florida have been created using the direct help of IMBA.

Alafia had a very different former life, one that most people would have difficulty envisioning, especially when compared to its modern appearance. Lands here were used for phosphate mining. During that time, they looked nothing like what you see here now. Alafia is what's called a reclaimed phosphate mine. Trees are replanted, earth is moved around, most large pits are backfilled, and the environment is restored as best as possible in most instances. Much of the intermediate and advanced trail make use of the old tailings left over from the mining process. Old mines are becoming familiar terrain for central and north Florida mountain bikers these days! Without their elevation changes, Florida mountain biking would be different altogether.

Novice riders, need not be alarmed however. Alafia has many miles of easier, well shaded trail and bypasses around many of the more technical areas.

Alafia River State Park's grand opening was held in concert with that of the mountain bike trail. This was held in December 2001, just in time for riders to take advantage of the long awaited cooler temperatures and long anticipated new trails!

At time of writing, a linkage trail between Alafia and nearby Balm-Boyette Scrub Preserve was still planned but not yet finished (see map for trail location and see Guide for Boyette). The trail makes use of a long abandoned railway corridor and provides a connection to even more adjacent trail mileage. The Tampa based SWAMP Club has done an incredible job of creating and maintaining these trails for our off-road bicycling pleasure. If you come across any local SWAMP'ers, be sure to thank them for their efforts!

Wildlife: Whitetail deer, feral hog, armadillo, rabbit, raccoon, opossum, turkey, endangered gopher tortoise, indigo snake, eastern diamond-back rattlesnake, scrub jay, red-shouldered hawk, red fox, swallowtail butterfly, rare Florida golden aster, etc.

Et cetera: Size: 5,458 acres. Hillsborough County. Hours: 8:00 a.m. to sunset year round. Helmets required. Park entrance fee. Bring plenty of food and water (several bottles and/ or a hydration pack). A map and compass are recommended as is a first-aid kit; know how to use each. Also bring a couple of spare tubes, a pump, any vital tools, a lightweight rain-coat, and insect repellent. This is a wild area encompassing thousands of acres. If you ride, you need to help maintain your trails. Contact SWAMP for trail work dates. Local food choices: Mexican in Wimauma and Burke & Howie's in Riverview. Tons more in Brandon.

When to Go: Fall, winter, and spring are the most enjoyable seasons to bike here, as they are cooler and much drier. There is little to no shade in the open prairie sections making them extremely hot and humid in the summer. However, luckily these sections are not very long. Keep hydrated and conserve your energy. Trail conditions are usually decent throughout the year, although with extremes of dryness or wetness, sandy sections or flooded/ muddy sections, respectively, can form. Slick clay is also probable during wet weather.

Contacts: Alafia River State Park, 14502 S. County Rd. 39, Lithia, FL 33547, (813) 672-5132; SWAMP Club: 9401 Takomah Trail, Tampa, FL 33617, (813) 985-5021. www.swampclub.org

Directions: From the north: take I-4 (if needed) to SR-39. Head south through Plant City and to SR-60. Continue south on 39 appx. 11 to 12 miles to park entrance on the left. If you hit CR-672 you've gone too far. . . . From the south: take I-75 to exit #240 (CR-674). Head east appx. 6 ½ miles, through Wimauma, then left onto Balm-Wimauma Rd. Head north several miles then turn right onto CR-672. Follow 672 east till you hit County Road 39. Take a left heading north. Park entrance is less than a mile on your right.

Sun-n-Lake Preserve

Location: Between Sebring and Avon Park

Managing Agency: Highlands County Parks and Recreation Department

Trail Length: Appx. 10 miles (not including southern doubletrack)

Difficulty: 90% beginner/intermediate; 10% advanced

Trail Type: 95% singletrack; 5% doubletrack

Description: This trail has been a work in progress since the late nineties. Nurtured to its current state by Dan Andrews and friends of Sebring's D&S Cycling Center, the trail now beckons fat tires to help finalize development. With more riders and increased popularity, The Preserve could easily fill in a conspicuous void of ride sites in this region of Florida. It "is" the only authorized singletrack for many miles in any direction!

Most of the trail development has been in the northern portion of the property. These trails are a mixed network of winding, flat, woodsy singletrack with a fun mid-section of undulating, tight trail making use of a small ridge. Most trails are marked with bright orange blazes and/ or orange marking tape on trees. However, they are not named or numbered. This means that it's easy to know if you're on "a" trail or not, but knowing precisely "which" trail is another matter. Signage should improve with time. The author also warns that the current trail map is conceptual in nature. Future Guide editions will contain a GPS'd map providing more accuracy.

Constituting the "10% advanced" level singletrack is an out-and-back trail in the northwest portion of the park (see map). This is a fun loop through tight, sinu-ous, hammocky terrain including several log overs, tree squeezes and small changes in elevation, often mid-turn. A few bends warranted trials-like nose-pivots to clean without dabbing. This section was obviously designed by a rider with technical in mind. Here, as with other sections, conditions will improve with more riders tamp-ing in the trail.

The southern loop (really in the middle of the property) has been ridden more and signed better. Orange arrows signal which way to ride. Several well-constructed wood bridges carry riders over small, tannic creeks. Picnic benches can be found just north of the intersecting doubletrack trail. These and the trail lie within a well shad-ed, slash pine overstory. This is a fun little trail. The southern portion of this loop makes use of a berm running along an old, overgrown dirt road. The trail leads up and down the thickly vegetated berm before banking back to the north. This is true for loops in either direction.

More trails are planned for the future. If you complete all of the current sin-gletrack and feel like getting more of a workout, explore the doubletrack trails in the middle and southern portions of the property. Most lead to back country ponds with further opportunities for wildlife observation (especially wading birds, alliga-tors, turtles, etc.).

Wildlife: Armadillo, raccoon, whitetail deer, opossum, bobcat, alligator and wading birds in lakes, various snakes, grey squirrel, turkey, etc. Flora consists of slash pine/ palmetto community and at least one alluring hammock dominated by cabbage palm and oak. This hammock is edged by a hardwood swamp.

Et cetera: Size: 1,350 acres. Highlands County. Helmets required. Hours: open 24 hours a day. Night riding at your own risk. No restrooms or facilities. Bring plenty of food and water (several bottles and/ or a hydration pack), first-aid kit and sun screen if desired. Also bring a couple of spare tubes, a pump and vital tools. Use trail map in Guide or obtain one at nearby D&S Cycling Center. No park entrance fee. Call Dan Andrews at D&S Cycling Center to ask about trail work days. If you ride, you need to help maintain your trails. . . . El Zarape III, on W. Main St. in downtown Avon Park, offers up local Mexican cuisine. The Cat House in downtown Sebring is a quirky restaurant geared toward the feline fanatic. Other restaurants and provisions along US-27. Historic Kenilworth Lodge in downtown Sebring caters to cyclists! They're used to us sweaty, dirty gear heads and will even store your bikes in a locked room upon request.

When to Go: Fall, winter, and spring are the most enjoyable seasons to bike here, as they are cooler and much drier. Portions of the trail can flood after heavy rains.

Contacts: D&S Cycling Center, 213 US Hwy 27 S., Sebring, (863) 382-7776. (The only bike shop around!); Highlands County Parks and Recreation Department, 4344 George Blvd., Sebring, FL 33875, (863) 402-6813.

Photo by Rebecca Tharrington

Riding the hammock loop at Sun-n-Lake Preserve

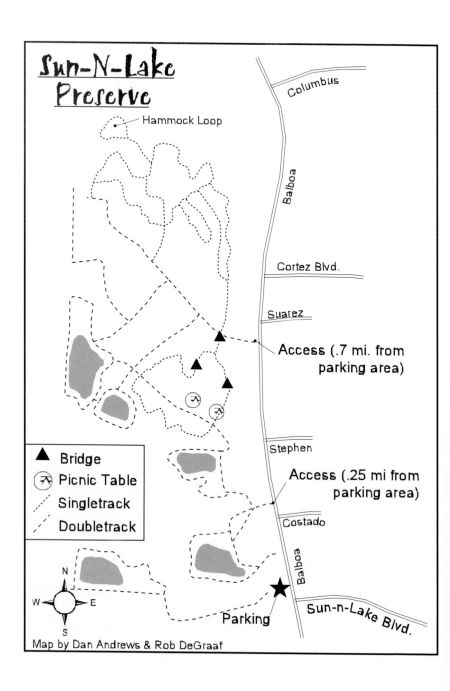

Sun-N-Lake Preserve

Columbus

Balboa

Hammock Loop

Cortez Blvd.

Suarez

Access (.7 mi. from parking area)

Stephen

Access (.25 mi from parking area)

Costado

Balboa

▲ Bridge
⊕ Picnic Table
Singletrack
Doubletrack

N
W   E
S

Parking

Sun-n-Lake Blvd.

Map by Dan Andrews & Rob DeGraaf

54

North Port Trail

Location: In North Port

Managing Agency: Sarasota County Parks and Recreation Department

Trail Length: Appx. 12 to 15 miles of trail. Several loop options possible

Difficulty: 30% beginner; 50% intermediate; 20% advanced

Trail Type: Mostly singletrack

Description: Myakkahatchee Creek, also known as Big Slough Canal, snakes southward toward the Myakka River. Along the way it passes an occasional mountainbiker, pedaling along its well-canopied banks. When cyclists stop for a breather they observe the swift, tannic stained water of the Creek flowing past.

Behind the handlebars one finds a trail that is sinuous, alluring and often challenging. Shaded singletrack beckons further exploration. The trail's difficulty ranges from novice to expert. Much of the trail includes an ample supply of roots and tight turns thrown in for good measure. Short, scrappy climbs and descents are common as are "gator-backs" and log-overs. The creek's banks range in height from just a couple feet to maybe 15 feet. A few sections of trail take cyclists right to the edge, literally, as they peer almost straight down into the paralleling creek.

Also interesting are several small canals/ dams that have to be crossed. The largest (see "Weir" on map) involves riding down a fairly steep cement embankment, through water in the bottom, and up the other side. Walking your bikes is of course a safe option to riding through these sections.

There are trails on both sides of the creek in most areas. The most common trailheads are shown on the map and are listed below. I say "most common" because this trail still has a bit of an un-manicured, wild feel to it. Many other access points exist but those shown here are on public property thus are "legal." Locals suggest riding the trail in a clockwise direction. Doing so, while not necessarily mandatory, is a good way to prevent serious head-on collisions on the trail's often tight, low visibility corners.

The trail is not frequently maintained compared to most other singletrack trails listed in the Guide. As such, you will find some surprises and increased technical as compared to some other sites.

Wildlife: Riverine habitat includes: river otter, turtles, alligator, water moccasin, myriad birds, etc.

Et cetera: Sarasota County. Helmets required. There are a couple of decent swim-holes along the creek. Be wary of water moccasins and alligators. As in many other areas of Florida, they may be present. Picnic tables at Lady Slipper trailhead. Myakkahatchee Environmental Center trailhead has restrooms, pavilions and a spigot for post ride cleanup. Price Blvd. trailhead has basic amenities. Seafood, etc., at Myakka River Oyster Bar on US-41 (Tamiami Trail), just west of the Myakka River/ bridge.

When to Go: Best seasons are fall, winter and spring. These months are cooler and drier. Creek can flood during extremely wet weather.

Contacts: Sarasota County Parks and Recreation Department, 6700 Clark Road, Sarasota, FL 34241, (941) 316-1172.

Directions: Several trailheads exist. All accessed from I-75, Exit # 182, Sumter Blvd . . . Northern trailhead: Myakkahatchee Creek Environmental Park: Sumter Blvd. north to left on Tropicaire Rd. Then right on Reisterstown Rd. Follow this to park entrance on the right. Follow trails on either side of creek south from here . . . Middle trailhead: Lady Slipper Avenue: Sumter Blvd. south to first right, onto Lady Slipper Ave. Drive .7 miles and look for small county park on the left . . . Southern trailhead: Price Blvd.: Sumter Blvd. south several miles to right on Price Blvd. Cross small bridge and look for park on left. Park here. Most head north from here on trails near bridge. Note: there is a lightly used, straight trail running south from Price Blvd., on west side of creek. It ends at Vestridge Street. This is a developed neighborhood and there is no public parking nearby. This trail segment may best be ridden as an out and back to increase mileage.

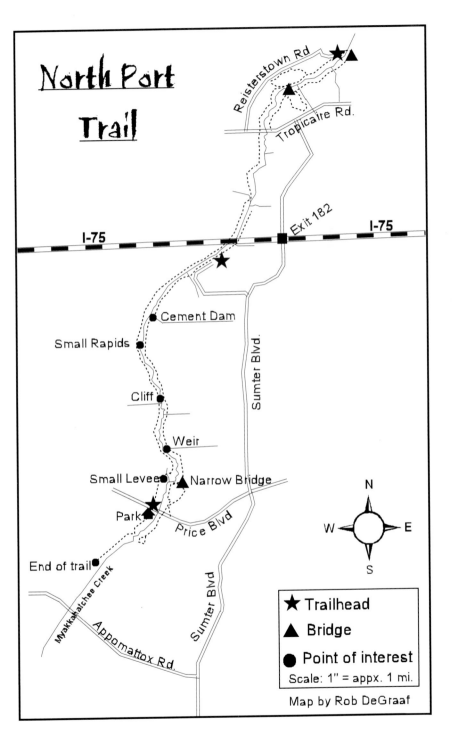

North Port Trail

Reisterstown Rd

Tropicaire Rd.

I-75   Exit 182   I-75

Cement Dam

Small Rapids

Cliff

Weir

Small Levee   Narrow Bridge

Park

Price Blvd

Sumter Blvd.

End of trail

Myakkahatchee Creek

Appomattox Rd.

Sumter Blvd

N
W   E
S

★ Trailhead
▲ Bridge
● Point of interest
Scale: 1" = appx. 1 mi.

Map by Rob DeGraaf

Miscellaneous Rides

Lochloosa Wildlife Conservation Area

Paynes Prairie Preserve State Park

Lower Suwannee National Wildlife Refuge

Andrews Wildlife Management Area

Manatee Springs State Park

Goethe State Forest

Silver River State Park

Ocklawaha Prairie Restoration Area

Sunnyhill Restoration Area

Emeralda Marsh Conservation Area

Lake Panasoffkee Wildlife Management Area

Potts Preserve Wildlife Management Area

Gum Slough & Half Moon WMAs

Withlacoochee State Forest – Homosassa Tract

Withlacoochee State Forest – Other Tracts

Chassahowitzka Wildlife Management Area

Green Swamp Wilderness Preserve

Upper Hillsborough Wildlife Management Area

Dead River Group Camp & Hillsborough River SP

Tenoroc Fish Management Area

Avon Park Air Force Range

Lochloosa Wildlife Conservation Area

Location: Between Ocala and Gainesville, near Hawthorne

Managing Agency: St. Johns River Water Management District and the Florida Fish and Wildlife Conservation Commission

Trail Length: Over 100 miles

Difficulty: Depends on speed and length of stay

Trail Type: 100% doubletrack

Description: Lochloosa is an elaborate labyrinth of old logging roads and ATV hunting trails. Trail surfaces range from hardpack to soft sand and pine needle cover. The main trails, noted on the map, are usually hardpack and relatively easy to ride unless logging vehicles and machinery have been used recently or after long dry spells. From the main trails, virtually countless numbers of side trails disperse. Some of these are beautifully arched with pines and have hardpack trail surfaces. At the other end of the continuum, some trails are freshly plowed fire breaks making them unpleasant for biking. Rainfall, while helping to pack down loose sand, can also leave some wet areas to cross.

One of the most appealing rides starts in the property's southeast corner, off of US-301, 1 ½ miles north of CR-325. This out-and-back trail heads northeast up a peninsula with Lochloosa Lake on three sides and includes a loop at the end. The lake views along the trail are incredible. You'll be hard pressed to see another person here outside of hunting season. This section is about 11-miles round trip if you don't investigate the numerous, tempting, side trails which can more than double this distance.

Lochloosa's ownership is vested with Georgia-Pacific. This timber company continues forestry operations on the property with specific restrictions. The St. Johns River Water Management District, who manages the land, owns a conservation easement that protects the property from ever being developed. The bottom line is that off-road bicyclists are welcome here except where logging operations cause temporary restrictions or trail closures due to safety concerns.

Wildlife: There are eighteen rare or endangered species here. A few of these include: black bear, gopher tortoise, fox squirrel, indigo snake, sandhill crane, bald eagle and wood stork. Whitetail deer and osprey are frequently seen. Flora consists of slash pine, planted in rows with varying maturities. Also to be found are turkey oak, beautyberry, palmetto, cabbage palm, live oak and many others.

Et cetera: Size: 27,327 acres. Alachua County. Hours: sunrise to sunset. Because there are so many intersecting roads it is easy to make a mistake and get lost. A compass, map, first aid kit and plenty of good judgement are preferred items here. Insect repellent is also recommended. Bring plenty of food and water (several bottles and/or a hydration pack). Also bring a couple of spare tubes, a pump, any vital tools and a lightweight rain-coat. This is a wild area encompassing thousands of acres. There are prescribed burns in sections. Fishing and canoeing are popular here. Except for a gated section in the southeast corner, north of Orange Lake, most roads on the property are open to motor vehicles. However, overall visitation is extremely light outside of hunting season . . . If time permits, ride the nearby Gainesville-Hawthorne State Trail (see map) . . . Also, nearby is the historic town of Cross Creek: location of the home of Florida author, Marjorie Kinnan Rollins.

When to Go: Ride early in the morning during the hot months. During cool weather, avoid hunt dates which are scattered from mid-September through mid-April. Contact Fish and Wildlife for a current hunt schedule before heading out.

Contacts: Florida Fish & Wildlife Conservation Commission, 620 S. Meridian St., Tallahassee, FL 32399, (850) 488-4676. On the web: www.state.fl.us/fwc; St. Johns River Water Management District, Division of Land Management, PO Box 1429, Palatka, FL 32178, (800) 451-7106. On the web: www.sjr.state.fl.us

Directions: There are numerous access points into Lochloosa. To get to the central trailhead, from I-75, take exit #368 (CR-318). Head east appx. 8 miles. Turn left, heading north, onto US-301. Continue 2 ½ miles then turn left onto CR-325. Follow 325 north to a left onto 346. Trailhead and kiosk are on the left . . . Other trailheads: Island Grove; on west side of US-301, 1 mi. north of CR-325. Security residence located here . . . Gainesville-Hawthorne State Trail: At least two access points into Lochloosa exist along this trail, which closely parallels CR-2082 here. One is just west of Hawthorne and the other is just east of CR-234 (see map). . . Another access point can be found on CR-346, appx. 4 mi. east of US-441, and 2 mi. east of CR-225. Look for parking and gate on south side of 346. Trail runs north and south from here. See map for more detail.

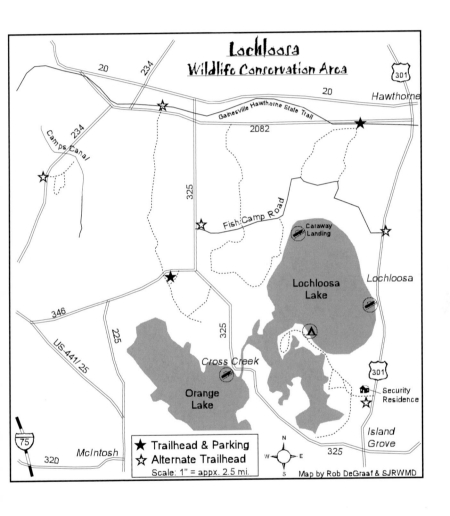

Lochloosa Wildlife Conservation Area

★ Trailhead & Parking
☆ Alternate Trailhead
Scale: 1" = appx. 2.5 mi.

Map by Rob DeGraaf & SJRWMD

Paynes Prairie Preserve State Park

Location: In Micanopy, south of Gainesville

Managing Agency: Florida Department of Environmental Protection, Division of Recreation and Parks

Trail Length: Appx. 15 miles, not including several return trips on out-and-back trails. Bolen Bluff trail is appx. 3 miles

Difficulty: 90% beginner; 10% intermediate (from occasional sugar sand, high grass or other trail obstructions)

Trail Type: 50% singletrack; 50% doubletrack (in open prairie sections)

Description: When a writer is faced with a combination of immensely rich cultural as well as natural history, such as that found at Paynes Prairie, two things occur: 1. He becomes extremely impressed with this fact, and 2. He comes to the realization that this diversity then has to be summarized as best as possible, as brief as possible, in writing. Writer ponders this for a moment, then decides he will instead head out for a long bike ride. . .

Over the years I have crossed Paynes Prairie many times. I-75 makes an apparent dip just south of Gainesville and suddenly, open, pasture-like terrain can be seen to the east and west of the highway. This "basin" was formed by the historical settling of the terrain and from the solution of the underlying limestone. Over the years the basin occasionally flooded forming a huge lake. In recent history the lake became large enough to support a steamboat service connecting several points in the area. Then, quite suddenly, nearby Alachua Sink became unplugged, essentially draining the huge lake. Like a fish out of water, the steamer was stranded and lay in its place for many years following this natural draining of the land.

Drier lands in the prairie meant better cattle grazing. The Camp and Bolen families in the early 1900's ran their cattle throughout the prairie. The Camps made a huge system of dikes and canals to reduce flooding. Many of these are still here and are now used for biking and hiking.

Most of the trail mileage is in very well shaded, upland forest. Geographically, better shade can be found in the southern and central sections of the park. Only when you enter the open prairie (in the north) do you encounter full sun. The author suggests riding the open sections during cooler months or dawn or dusk in summer. Moreover, avoiding these open prairie trails means missing a chance to see wild bison and Spanish horses which, before human settlement, used to roam here. Reintroduced in the 1970's and 80's, they again graze freely throughout the prairie but are very few in number.

One steamy summer morning, on my first ride of the Bolen Bluff trail (see directions), a friend and I came across four bison grazing alongside the dike. We were pleasantly surprised. These animals are huge and riders should maintain a respectful distance during an encounter. What are the chances of seeing bison here? Pretty slim. In 2001 there were just seven roaming the prairie's thousands of acres. The four I saw are sisters and tend to stick together. A ranger informed me that some staff, after years of service at the park, have yet to see the animals. I was incredibly lucky, yet this luck was combined with riding before 8:00 a.m., when the trails were empty, and riding very quietly to increase my chances of success.

Trail side notes: enjoyed the shady, slightly rolling terrain of Jackson's Gap trail. Look for the multi-story abandoned home along this trail. To the north, on Cone's Dike, a huge doe crossed the trail in front of me. Many butterflies and damselflies are also along this trail. Back east at the Chacala Pond Overlook, a small alligator and many wading birds were observed along the pond's edge. Later, while heading to Gainesville, we walked out on the short boardwalk from US-441. Just a few minutes of viewing yielded marsh rabbit, turtle, leopard frog, purple gallinule with chicks, and a wide diversity of plant life.

<u>Wildlife</u>: I'd probably save a lot of space here by listing those plants and animals which are absent from Paynes Prairie: there are notably very few. Chances are, if you've seen or heard about it in Florida, you'll find it here. Moreover, there are several oddities as well. The park overflows with biodiversity. Many rare or endangered species and ecosystems are found here. From the somewhat common: whitetail deer, bobcat, otter, alligator, various hawks, wading birds, sandhill cranes, snakes, frogs, etc... To the very rare: reintroduced Spanish horse and American bison. Very few of the latter roam about the prairie. Dawn or dusk explorations usually yield increased wildlife sightings ... To be found are: pine flatwoods, hardwood hammock, swamps, lakes and ponds, and the huge wet prairie or basin – the central feature of the park.

<u>Et cetera</u>: Size: 21,000 acres. Alachua County. Hours: sunrise to sunset. Bring plenty of food and water (several bottles and/ or a hydration pack). A map and compass are recommended as is a first-aid kit; know how to use each. Also bring a couple of spare tubes, a pump, any vital tools, a lightweight rain-coat, and insect repellent. This is a wild area encompassing thousands of acres... Note: Map for Bolen Bluff trail not included here. Map at trailhead is sufficient and trail is very easy to follow. The short boardwalk trail on US-441 is worth a side trip.

Other park activities include: hiking, camping, fishing, non-motorized boating and paddling in Wauberg Lake, nature study, horseback riding, picnicking, etc... Other activities around the area include: paved cycling on the 16 mile Gainesville-Hawthorne Rail Trail, Kanapaha Botanical Gardens, Devil's Millhopper State Geological Site, etc. Ask park staff for a "Vicinity map" showing other points of interest... Lodging can be found in Micanopy (well known Herlong mansion and at least one other B&B) or on a budget at motel near 75. Otherwise, head north into Gainesville. Camping is pleasant during cooler months... At time of writing, nearby food choices were: Kismet Garden Café, east of park on 441, and a hamburger joint further east still. Downtown Micanopy had snacks but no restaurants. Head north on 441 into Gainesville to increase your food options.

<u>When to Go</u>: Fall, winter, and spring are the most enjoyable seasons to bike here,

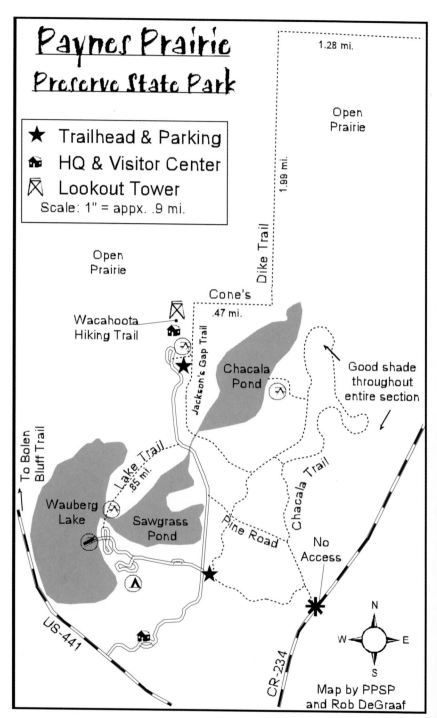

as they are cooler and drier. Open prairie sections (like Cone's Dike Trail) are brutal in the summer. Grass becomes very thick, as does the humidity! Keep hydrated and conserve your energy. Overall, trail conditions are usually decent throughout the year, although with extremes of dryness or wetness, sandy sections or flooded/ muddy sections, respectively, can form..

<u>Contacts:</u> Paynes Prairie Preserve State Park, 100 Savannah Blvd., Micanopy, FL 32667, (352) 466-3397.

<u>Directions:</u> To all trailheads inside park: From I-75: Exit 374. Head east on CR-234. Follow bypass around Micanopy to US-441. Make left heading north. Park entrance will be appx. 1 mile on your right. To Bolen Bluff Trail: Following directions above, head 2 - 3 miles past park entrance continuing north on US-441. Trailhead and parking area will be on your right before 441 crosses the prairie basin. From Gainesville: Head south on US-441, cross the prairie, and look for Bolen's Bluff trailhead on your left. Entrance to the State Park is 2 -3 miles further south, also on the left.

Lower Suwannee National Wildlife Refuge

Location: Near Cedar Key, Chiefland and Cross City

Managing Agency: U.S. Fish and Wildlife Service

Trail Length: 90 miles, several separate tracts

Difficulty: Depends on speed and length of stay

Trail Type: Doubletrack and other dirt roads

Description: With this amount of trail mileage, one could explore here for weeks or longer without seeing the same thing twice. Put simply, the place is gigantic. Add to this the lack of back country campsites and you have a place where thorough exploring requires many, full day, epic rides. Two county campgrounds exist nearby: Shired Island in the north (on map) and Shell Mound in the south (at end of CR-326). Luckily, there are dozens of trailheads, accessed by 40 miles of dirt roads open to vehicles. The additional 50 miles of roads open to bicyclists are accessed, for the most part, from the vehicular roads.

The beautiful and historic Suwannee River splits the Refuge in half. The closest bridge crossing, however, is at US-19/ 98 near Fanning Springs. Therefore, driving from one parcel to the other is a lengthy affair. The best idea is to focus on one section at a time. Spend a weekend in the north, then next time, stay in the south. This keeps you on the bike longer and in the car less!

The Refuge was established in 1979 to preserve the Suwannee River delta and estuary. With 26 miles of frontage on the Gulf, the Refuge is one of the largest, most ecologically valuable, river-delta ecosystems in the U.S. Since the Refuge is so large, wild and remote, wildlife thrives here. Black bear, requiring large, contiguous tracts of wilderness, reside here. Two-hundred fifty-four bird species have been observed here. Many nest on the outlying, isolated islands of nearby Cedar Keys National Wildlife Refuge, then come to Lower Suwannee to feed.

Most of the roads and trails are hardpack: lime rock, clay, and other woods roads. Vehicular roads, also open to bikes, are much more well worn than the 50 miles of trail open to bikers and hikers. Conditions can vary greatly, so be prepared for just about anything. The main dirt road in the north is called the Dixie Mainline Trail. It connects CR-349 in the south with CR-357 to the north. Nine miles in length, it is a scenic, lime rock, interpretive road leading through several ecosystems, including the enticing California Swamp. It is open to slow-moving vehicles, but usage is extremely light. The trail makes use of an old tram road (railroad) corridor used off and on from the 1920's to the 1960's by the timber industry. Ironically, this very route is now used to showcase the preservation of the same woods that were once looked at merely for their economic value. Several bridges cross scenic, tidally influenced streams and marshland. These were finished in 1998; built to replace the old, dilapidated wood bridges left by the logging companies. Several interesting off shoot roads and trails leave the Dixie Mainline, some open only to bikes and those on foot. Other dirt roads open to bicyclists in the northern section include those off CR-349. Several trails head off into the back country from here, several leading down to views of the nearby Suwannee River. See map.

In the southern tract there is a main dirt road that runs north - south through the parcel. Thirteen miles south of Chiefland, on CR-347, look on west side of the road for North Entrance Gate 1. It is well marked. This road winds south, roughly 10 miles, before coming back out to 347 at gate 9. There are dozens of off shoot trails from this road, all of which are open to bicyclists. See map. The Refuge headquarters is accessed from Gate 1.

You may want to consider using a Global Positioning System (GPS) here if you have one. Rob uses a Garmin GPS II+ mounted to his handlebars. Just be sure to back up your GPS with a standard compass in case you lose battery power or destroy your GPS in the back country. See the Introduction for more navigating tips.

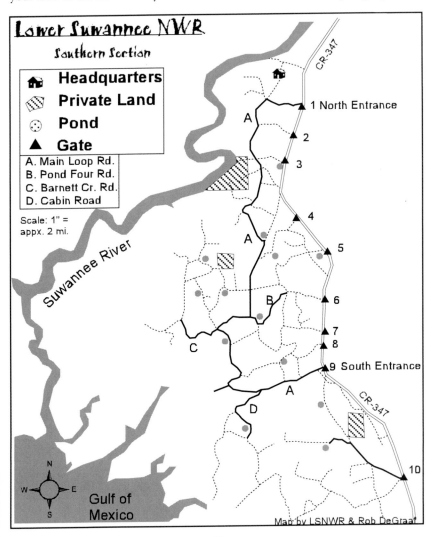

Lower Suwannee NWR
Southern Section

Headquarters
Private Land
Pond
Gate

A. Main Loop Rd.
B. Pond Four Rd.
C. Barnett Cr. Rd.
D. Cabin Road

Scale: 1" = appx. 2 mi.

Suwannee River

CR-347

1 North Entrance
2
3
4
5
6
7
8
9 South Entrance

CR-347

10

Gulf of Mexico

Map by LSNWR & Rob DeGraat

Wildlife: Winter and spring are the best seasons for wildlife observation. Florida black bear are present but seldom seen. Also, grey fox, grey squirrel, whitetail deer, feral hog, turkey, armadillo, otter, alligator, raccoon, etc. 254 bird species, including nesting bald eagle, osprey and swallow-tailed kite (ask the Refuge for the complete checklist). Marine mammals such as bottlenose dolphin, endangered West Indian Manatee, several species of marine turtles, and more. A few endangered whooping cranes winter here. These were introduced in 2001. Various ecosystems include: hardwood hammock, tidal marsh, delta-estuary, cypress dominated flood plain hardwood swamp, upland slash pine/ palmetto community, scrub oak, etc.

Et cetera: Size: 52,935 acres. Dixie and Levy Counties. Refuge office hours are from 7:30 a.m. to 4:00 p.m. No camping or fires on Refuge. Bring plenty of food and water (several bottles and/ or a hydration pack). A map, compass and GPS are recommended as is a first-aid kit; know how to use each. Also bring a couple of spare tubes, a pump and any vital tools. Insect repellent, sun screen, and rain gear also suggested. This is a wild area encompassing thousands of acres so be prepared. In the summer, bug severity here rivals that found in the Everglades! Without repellent you are lunch! Hunting is permitted typically in the winter. Call the Refuge for exact dates.

Other nearby activities and sites include: surprise, more biking! See Andrews WMA and Manatee Springs SP (separate writeups) and Cedar Key Scrub State Preserve (Honorable Mention section). Hiking any of the above sites, including Shell Mound and Dennis Creek trails (at end of CR-326) within the Refuge. Shell Mound was created by Timucan Indians over 3,500 years ago and is the largest, highest mound on the Gulf. Fresh and saltwater fishing are popular all over the region, as is swimming, snorkeling and SCUBA diving in local springs including Manatee and Fanning. Many others flow into the Suwannee River and are shown in good maps such as DeLorme's Florida Atlas and Gazetteer. If you like wine, or if you think you don't, stop in at Dakotah Winery, on US-19, Chiefland. Florida muscadine grapes make a great tasting wine in my opinion. BBQ Bill's serves up some decent BBQ and is open for breakfast. Town of Cedar Key is loaded with interesting history, lodging, great dining, antiquing and other shopping. History museum is worth a trip. Staying (and playing) here is a more attractive choice than nearby Chiefland.

When to Go: Fall, winter, and spring are the most enjoyable seasons to bike here, as they are cooler, drier and much less buggy.

Contacts: Refuge Manager, Lower Suwannee National Wildlife Refuge, 16450 Northwest 31 Place, Chiefland, FL 32626, (352) 493-0238. On the web at: www.fws.gov/r4eao or www.fws.gov/r4swe ; The U.S. Fish and Wildlife Service can be reached at: 1-800-344-WILD.

Directions: Northern Tract: To northern terminus of Dixie MainlineTrail: take CR-351A south from Cross City at US-19. This becomes CR-351. Follow south then make left onto CR-357. Continue south appx. 7 ½ miles then look for the trail on your left. To southern terminus of Dixie MainlineTrail: take CR-349 south from

Old Town at US-19. Head appx. 20 miles south as you "carefully" watch for trailhead on your right. If you hit town of Suwannee, you've gone a couple miles too far. . . . Southern Tract: To North Entrance Gate 1 (and Refuge HQ): 4 miles south of Chiefland, from US-19, take CR-347 west appx. 13 miles. Gate and Refuge HQ are well marked, on the right (west) side of road. Gate 9, which is the other terminus of this dirt road, is located around 5 miles to the south, also on west side of CR-347. It is also well marked.

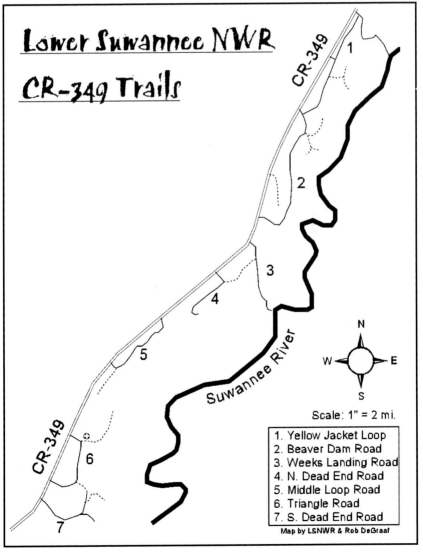

Lower Suwannee NWR
CR-349 Trails

Suwannee River

CR-349

CR-349

N
W — E
S

Scale: 1" = 2 mi.

1. Yellow Jacket Loop
2. Beaver Dam Road
3. Weeks Landing Road
4. N. Dead End Road
5. Middle Loop Road
6. Triangle Road
7. S. Dead End Road

Map by LSNWR & Rob DeGraaf

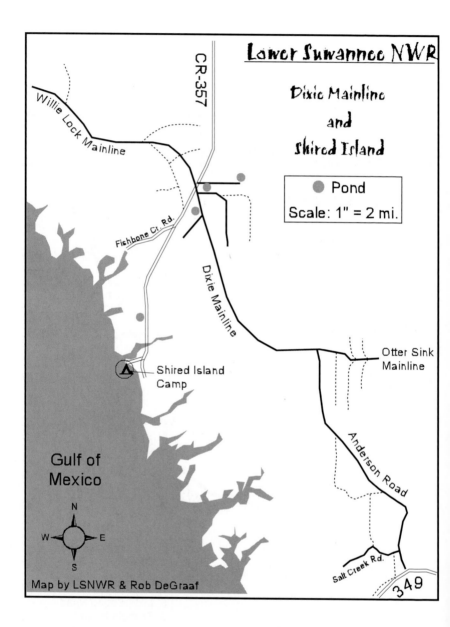

Lower Suwannee NWR

Dixie Mainline
and
Shired Island

● Pond
Scale: 1" = 2 mi.

CR-357

Willie Lock Mainline

Fishbone Cr. Rd.

Dixie Mainline

Otter Sink Mainline

Anderson Road

▲ Shired Island Camp

Gulf of Mexico

N
W E
S

Salt Creek Rd.

349

Map by LSNWR & Rob DeGraaf

Dixie Mainline trail - Lower Suwannee NWR

Photo by Rob DeGraaf

Andrews Wildlife Management Area

Location: North of Chiefland

Managing Agency: Florida Fish and Wildlife Conservation Commission (FF&WCC) and Suwannee River Water Management District (SRWMD)

Trail Length: More than 15 miles

Difficulty: Depends on speed and length of stay

Trail Type: Doubletrack and other dirt roads

Description: Andrews Wildlife Management Area (WMA) is quite a gem. It is arguably the largest remaining hardwood forest on the lower Suwannee river. What does this mean for off-road bicyclists? Lots of shade and hardpack riding conditions! Towering oak, sweetgum, birch, elm, basswood, maple, and others make up the forest overstory. Many of these are so called "Champion Trees," holding size records for their particular species. At least half a dozen, yellow-blazed spur trails to these trees lead off from other dirt roads. These trails are among the most rugged routes on the property since they are very lightly traveled. They are enjoyable at the same time they are somewhat precarious: it is very easy to get lost here. The WMA is lightly visited. Bring a friend or two and plan ahead. Help may be a long way off.

Consider using a Global Positioning System (GPS) here if you have one. Some trails are poorly marked and maintained, especially once you're on them. Finding these trails may not be a problem. Following them, or linking to other sections of the property, however, can be more of a challenge. Rob uses a Garmin GPS II+ mounted to his handlebars. Just be sure to back up your GPS with a standard compass in case you lose battery power or destroy your GPS in the back country. See the Introduction for more navigating tips.

Wildlife is abundant. However, unfortunately, this includes ticks, biting flies and plenty of mosquitoes. Load up on insect repellent, consider wearing high socks or lightweight pants, and do "tick checks" post ride! Now that I have played Mr. Mom by giving countless warnings, let's get back to the trail description.

With many various trailheads, accessed from many miles of dirt roads open to vehicles and bicycles, countless ride options exist. The best way to see the property may be to choose a centrally located trailhead, leave your vehicle, and ride loops from there. Parking locations are prevalent as long as your vehicle is not blocking a road or gate. Fort Fanning Road runs north - south through the property's central spine. It, like almost every road here, is shady, hardpack, scenic doubletrack. Parking at the river picnic areas on either Buckeye Trail or Turkey Track Trail provide unmatched scenery and offer a central location for several loop rides. Dick's Slough Road in the south is a nice, rolling, doubletrack ride leading to secluded views of the Suwannee River (via short connector trail). It also provides access to several "Champion Tree" trails. A great loop can be ridden from the north end of Fort Fanning Road. Head north past gate, then bear left, then left again heading south (using that compass I

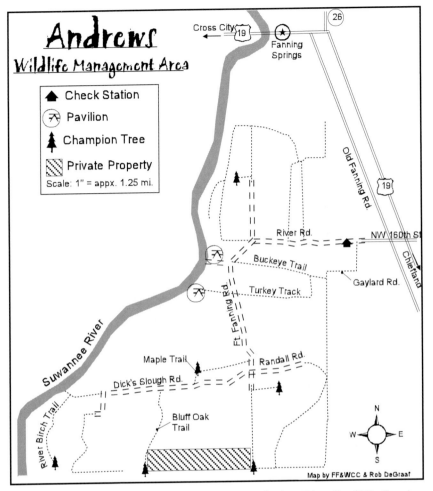

Map by FF&WCC & Rob DeGraaf

suggested). Continue south to a left on trail leading back to River Road/ Ft. Fanning Rd. intersection (see map). Many sinkholes can be sighted from this loop as well as other trails. There is an old tram road that parallels the river, to the west of these roads. It is somewhat tough to find and is a rugged, dead-end trail, terminating suddenly at a hardwood swamp almost as far south as River Rd. Mosquitoes can be very thick on this section of trail.

<u>Wildlife:</u> Florida black bear may be present but is seldom seen. Also, grey fox, grey squirrel, fox squirrel, whitetail deer, feral hog, bobcat, skunk, otter, turkey, armadillo, raccoon, etc. Flora consists of oak (several varieties), maple, sweetgum, river birch, basswood, elm, magnolia, bald cypress, slash pine, palmetto, sparkleberry, occasional paw paw, etc.

<u>Et cetera:</u> Size: 3,501 acres. Levy County. Hours: from ½ before sunrise to ½ hour after sunset. No camping. Bring plenty of food and water (several bottles and/ or a

hydration pack). A map, compass and GPS are recommended as is a first-aid kit; know how to use each. Also bring a couple of spare tubes, a pump and any vital tools. Insect repellent, sun screen, and rain gear also suggested. This is a wild area encompassing thousands of acres so be prepared. In the summer, bugs are fierce! Hunting is permitted typically in the winter. Call FF&WCC for exact dates.

Other nearby activities and sites include: surprise, more biking! See Lower Suwannee NWR and Manatee Springs SP (separate writeups) and Cedar Key Scrub State Preserve (Honorable Mention section). Hiking any of the above sites, including Shell Mound and Dennis Creek trails (at end of CR-326) within Lower Suwannee NWR. Shell Mound was created by Timucan Indians over the course of 3,500 years, and is the largest, highest mound on the Gulf. Fresh and saltwater fishing are popular all over the region, as is swimming, snorkeling and SCUBA diving in local springs including Manatee and Fanning. Many others flow into the Suwannee River and are shown in good maps such as DeLorme's Florida Atlas and Gazetteer. If you like wine, or if you think you don't, stop in at Dakotah Winery, on US-19, Chiefland. Florida muscadine grapes make a great tasting wine in my opinion. BBQ Bill's serves up some decent BBQ and is open for breakfast. Town of Cedar Key is loaded with interesting history, lodging, great dining, antiquing and other shopping. History museum is worth a trip. Staying (and playing) here is a more attractive choice than nearby Chiefland.

When to Go: Fall, winter, and spring are the most enjoyable seasons to bike here, as they are cooler, drier and much less buggy.

Contacts: Florida Fish & Wildlife Conservation Commission, 620 S. Meridian St., Tallahassee, FL 32399, (850) 488-4676. On the web at: www.state.fl.us/fwc or Suwannee River Water Management District, 9225 CR-49, Live Oak, FL 32060; (800) 226-1066. On the web at: www.srwmd.state.fl.us

Directions: From US-19, Chiefland: head appx. 5 ½ miles north to 160th Street. Make left heading west. Cross Old Fanning Road and the Nature Coast Rail-Trail. Kiosk, maps and other information are straight ahead at property entrance. Many of the dirt roads on the property are open to vehicles.

River Birch trail - Andrews WMA   *Photo by Rob DeGraaf*

Manatee Springs State Park

Location: Near Chiefland

Managing Agency: Florida Department of Environmental Protection, Division of Recreation and Parks

Trail Length: 8.5 miles in the north and more in the south

Difficulty: Depends on speed and length of stay

Trail Type: Doubletrack and other dirt roads

Description: I stopped here to ride one day after already logging some serious mileage at nearby Andrews WMA to the north. I was hot and ready for a swim. My initial expectation was that there would be just a few short, semi-interesting trails that I could quickly explore before heading over to the spring for a refreshing plunge. Well, I still got to swim, but by the time I did I had logged even more mileage on Manatee's trails and dirt roads. What I found here impressed me. Thickly wooded, shady, hardpack, doubletrack roads comprise the park's "North Trail System" affording decent mileage and great scenery. The trails are twisty and slightly rolling in a few sections, and bring cyclists within view of a few small sinkholes here and there.

The trails are very well marked. Park trail maps are accurate and a couple back country trail kiosks have been placed to further facilitate navigation. Many public lands and parks I have been on could learn much from what the folks at Manatee have done with their trail system. The best example of this is demonstrated by the method in which the park measured their trails. Using FDOT road measuring wheels, each trail segment was individually surveyed and mapped. This is uncommon to say the least, and very much appreciated by bicyclists.

Ask park staff about the trail system in the southern portion of property. I was informed that there was more mileage there than in the north but that the trails were not very well marked or measured yet. However, they are open for bicycling but you need to speak to park staff first.

Manatee Spring is huge: first magnitude in size, flowing 81,280 gallons per minute, approximately 117 million gallons daily. It is around 30 feet deep to the vent. Deeper once inside (for divers). Water so clear, myriad fish like mullet and bass are seen, as are SCUBA divers lingering below in the rejuvenating, 72 degree water. The flow is so strong, swimming underwater toward the vent is akin to swimming upstream in a raging river. From here the water flows into the nearby Suwannee River, which then flows 23 miles downstream before reaching the Gulf of Mexico. Be sure to check out the boardwalk trail through hardwood swamp, paralleling the spring run leading out to the Suwannee River. Fish, wading birds and turtles are commonly seen. If your timing is good, you may glimpse a West Indian Manatee near the confluence of the spring and river, or see a sturgeon rolling or jumping in the Suwannee. Ask park staff for best times/ seasons for viewing wildlife.

In my opinion, this is what Florida mountain-biking is all about: being able to combine fun off-road bicycling with great swimming opportunities like that found at Manatee Springs.

Wildlife: Grey squirrel, fox squirrel, whitetail deer, feral hog, bobcat, skunk, otter, turkey, armadillo, raccoon, etc. Sturgeon and West Indian Manatee in nearby Suwannee River. Flora consists of oak (several varieties), maple, sweetgum, ash, elm, magnolia, bald cypress, loblolly, slash and long leaf pine, saw palmetto, sparkleberry, etc.

Et cetera: Size: 2,075 acres. Levy County. Hours: 9:00 am to sunset all year. Park entrance fee. Other park activities include camping, hiking, paddling (canoe rentals in park), swimming, snorkeling and SCUBA diving in spring, and fishing in Suwannee River accessed via boardwalk along spring run. Bring plenty of food and water (several bottles and/ or a hydration pack). A map and compass are recommended as is a first-aid kit; know how to use each. Also bring a couple of spare tubes, a pump and any vital tools. Insect repellent and sun screen also suggested. Ticks and chiggers may be a problem, so load up on insect repellent before heading out. Post ride, be sure to check for ticks.

Other nearby activities and sites include: surprise, more biking! See Lower Suwannee NWR and Andrews WMA (separate writeups) and Cedar Key Scrub State Preserve (Honorable Mention section). Hiking any of the above sites, including Shell Mound and Dennis Creek trails (at end of CR-326) within Lower Suwannee NWR. Shell Mound was created by Timucan Indians over the course of 3,500 years, and is the largest, highest mound on the Gulf. Fresh and saltwater fishing are popular all over the region, as is swimming, snorkeling and SCUBA diving in local springs including Manatee here and Fanning to the north. Many others flow into the Suwannee River and are shown in good maps such as DeLorme's Florida Atlas and Gazetteer. If you like wine, or if you think you don't, stop in at Dakotah Winery, on US-19, Chiefland. Florida muscadine grapes make a great tasting wine in my opinion. BBQ Bill's serves up some decent BBQ and is open for breakfast. Town of Cedar Key is loaded with interesting history, lodging, great dining, antiquing and other shopping. History museum is worth a trip. Staying (and playing) here is a more attractive choice than nearby Chiefland.

When to Go: Fall, winter, and spring are the most enjoyable seasons to bike here, as they are cooler, drier and much less buggy. However, even in the summer, the cool refreshing waters of Manatee Springs await as reward for long, hot rides.

Contacts: Manatee Springs State Park, 11650 NW 115th Street, Chiefland, FL 32626, (352) 493-6072

Directions: From US-19, Chiefland: head appx. 1 mile north of town on US-19. Take left heading west on CR-320. Park entrance is appx. 6 miles down 320. At gate, ask a ranger for directions to North End Trail System. Also ask about status of trails in south section.

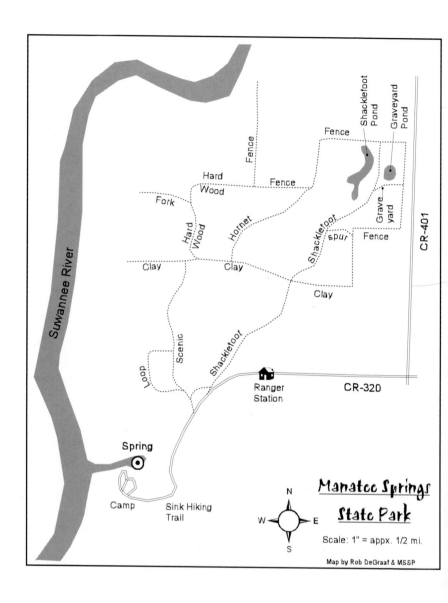

Manatee Springs
State Park

Scale: 1" = appx. 1/2 mi.

Map by Rob DeGraaf & MSSP

Goethe State Forest &
Wildlife Management Area

Location: Between Inglis and Williston in southeastern Levy County

Managing Agency: Florida Department of Agriculture and Consumer Services, Division of Forestry and Florida Fish and Wildlife Conservation Commission

Trail Length: More than 200 miles

Difficulty: 20% beginner; 80% intermediate

Trail Type: 100% double track

Description: Goethe State Forest is named for Mr. J. T. Goethe from whom most of the land was purchased under Florida's Conservation and Recreation Lands (CARL) Program in 1992. There are about 40 miles of improved roads with hardened lime rock surfaces that are easy riding for even the beginner. Many riders prefer these surfaces as little effort produces great scenery, good speed and a slight breeze. Beyond this, there are more than 160 miles of connecting service roads open to off-road bicyclists. These same roads are closed to motor vehicles. These trails, while having mostly firm surfaces often have thick grass. This makes travel somewhat slow and requires a lower gear. There are some water crossings, especially in the southern, Tidewater area.

The forest is an equestrian haven and they have a well organized and well marked trail system using colored trail markers. Bikers will find these trails frequently shifting between improved roads and service roads and the first mile or two from a trailhead gets lots of horse traffic making the biking here difficult and sometimes unpleasant. You may want to stick to the improved roads near trailheads. Once you've pedaled in a little ways, conditions typically improve. A great place to start a ride here is at the Black Prong trailhead, riding either the red (circle) or the orange (diamond) trails which are about 8 miles each. Black Prong Road and Cow Creek Road also offer a great north-south view of the forest on relatively untraveled roads.

The southern two-thirds of Goethe has expansive stands of longleaf pine with tall straight trunks and green tufted tops. The understory is a sea of thick palmetto. Views from most of the roads reach deep and unobstructed (other than bare tree trunks) into this interesting landscape and usually end at the more dense cypress domes or bay heads. The northern one-third of the forest is predominantly hardwoods. Unless you're a skilled environmental scientist, you will find it difficult to differentiate the more than 15 distinct natural communities such as scrubby flatwoods, dome swamp, sand hill and basin swamp. Of course, this doesn't mean you won't appreciate the scenery.

Goethe contains the largest acreage of contiguous, old-growth longleaf pine flatwoods in the state with several trees over 200 years old. Part of the importance of this is that the rare, red-cockaded woodpecker will only nest in the hollows of old-growth pine trees. Thus, having so many large specimens to choose from means that the forest can maintain one of the highest populations of woodpeckers in the state. Biologists have painted white rings around the trunks of trees with hollows that these birds tend to use. Finding a white ring increases your chances of seeing woodpeckers. As you enter a red-cockaded woodpecker area there is a vertical white paint mark on the perimeter trees and as you exit the area you will see a white circle on the perimeter trees.

There are many disconnected sections of the forest, each with its own name and trail map. Their names and trail side notes follow (from north to south): Black Prong Trails: Alternate forest office and fire-tower on CR-343 near Black Prong Rd. Blue trail decent. Most other trails hardpack. Cow Creek Trails: Mostly hardpack. Beautiful flatwoods. Apex Trails: Mostly flatwoods terrain. Daniel's Island Trails: Forest HQ on CR-336, just east of US-19 and SR-121. Some wet, swampy areas mixed with higher, hammocky sections. Old cabin off Ten Mile Rd. Forestry Youth Academy off Glass Rd. Tidewater (AKA Stein) Trails: Yellow short loop very sandy. Call for status of other loops here. Call contact number listed below to obtain current trail maps and section updates.

Wildlife: Most frequently spotted wildlife include deer, gopher tortoise, fox squirrel and the endangered red-cockaded woodpecker. Other rare species that call this home include the Florida black bear and bald eagle. Rare plants include the hooded pitcher plant and coontie.

Et cetera: Size: 50,172 acres. Alachua and Levy Counties. Hours: sunrise to sunset. Hunt schedules are published annually with archery starting in late September and the spring turkey hunt ending in late March, but there are numerous dates between these when no hunting is permitted. Be sure to obtain a hunt schedule if you plan to ride in these cooler months. Horses are easily spooked by bikers so speak to the rider when approaching and request permission to pass. Dismounting may be required on narrow trail sections.

When to Go: Even though the trails are sparsely shaded, the abundance of tall trees keeps the area relatively cool (compared to non-forested areas) so one can enjoy trips here almost any time of the year. Just remember to avoid riding during a scheduled hunt.

Contacts: Goethe State Forest, 8250 SE County Road 336, Dunnellon, FL 34431. Phone: (352) 447-2202. On the web: www.fl-dof.com ; Florida Fish & Wildlife Conservation Commission, 620 S. Meridian St., Tallahassee, FL 32399, (850) 488-4676. On the web: www.state.fl.us/fwc

Directions: To get to Forest HQ, from the north on I-75, take SR-121 south into Williston. Turn right at Alt. 27 (Noble Ave.). Left on US-41 for 1 mile. Then right on SR-121 again. Follow 121 till it ends at Lebanon. Make left onto CR-336 and look for park office on the left. . . From the south on I-75, take exit #352 (SR-40). Head west into Dunnellon staying on 40 as it curves through town. A few miles west of town, turn right onto CR-336. Follow 336 appx. 10 miles as you watch for the park office on your left. If you hit US-98, you've gone too far. . . With many disconnected sections of the forest, giving directions becomes somewhat complicated. First, obtain a good map, like DeLorme's Florida Atlas. Second, provided here are general locations of offices and main trailheads: Forest HQ: on CR-336, just east of US-19 and SR-121. . . Alternate forest office and fire-tower: On east side of CR-343, north of CR-326, near Black Prong Rd. . . Black Prong Trailhead: At Camp Road. This is on west side of CR-337, a couple miles north of CR-326. . . Cow Creek Trailhead: At Cow Creek Rd. or Woodpecker Rd., which intersect CR-326 in the north, between CR-337 and CR-343. South access at Cow Creek Rd. at SR-121. . . Apex Trailhead: At Gas Line Rd. This is on west side of CR-337, just south of SR-121. . . Daniel's Island Trailhead: At Old Rock Rd. at intersection of CR-337 and 336. Also at Gas Line Rd., west of CR-337 on 336. . . Tidewater (AKA Stein) Trailhead: At Saddle Pen Rd. off of CR-337, just north of CR-336 and 337 intersection. There may be other access along CR-336. Call the Forest for details.

Old cabin on Ten Mile Road

Photo by Rob DeGraaf

Silver River State Park

Location: East of Ocala and south of Silver Springs

Managing Agency: Florida Department of Environmental Protection, Division of Recreation and Parks

Trail Length: 13 miles

Difficulty: 70% beginner; 30% intermediate

Trail Type: 15% singletrack; 85% doubletrack

Description: The cool, clear river that emerges from one of Florida's largest artesian springs, runs directly into Silver River State Park. Silver Springs, churning out 530 million gallons per day, flows approximately 4 miles through the park before emptying into the dark, tannin-stained waters of the Ocklawaha River. This water comes from one main spring vent and over a dozen smaller, adjacent springs. Over three miles of the Ocklawaha lie within the eastern portion of the park. The park's trails allow you to view the picturesque Silver River from numerous points. One of these provides an opportunity to swim. It should be noted that while much of the river bottom is sandy, the shore line, consisting of lightly colored clay, is very slick. Therefore, be careful as you step into the swift, cool water. Also, be on the lookout for alligators. Once, on a canoe trip up and down the river, we spotted more than 60 alligators.

Bicycles are permitted on all trails within the park. Of the 13 miles of trails, some are easier to ride than others. Trails on the west side are often sandy, thus afford more enjoyable riding on or after rainy days. Trails that reach the river from the museum area and those that are near the swimming area have mostly a hard, lime rock surface. When dry, these are easy trails for beginners. When wet, however, the algae and moss growing on the surface make conditions very slick, almost as slick as a frozen lake. If your tires start to slide it's probably too late! Even putting your foot down may be useless as it too will slide. Ride slowly and carefully over slippery sections of trail. Tread ever so lightly and do not turn suddenly.

The trails are heavily shaded and wind through oak and palm forest of stunning beauty. Interpretive signs along the trail educate the reader/ rider about numerous species of plants. These informative signs afford a good opportunity for the cyclist to expand his or her knowledge of Florida's natural communities. Doing so in turn lends to an increased appreciation for native Florida ecosystems.

The eastern portion of the park includes twisting singletrack leading through a verdant, jungle like forest: Ft. King Military and Long Field are 100% singletrack and Ross Allen Camp Trail is mixed single and doubletrack. These trails were developed for the park by the Ocala Mountain Biking Association (OMBA) and are being expanded. Skilled riders will really enjoy navigating this section. If you see an OMBA volunteer on the trails be sure to thank them for all their hard work.

Wildlife: Fifteen distinct natural communities have been identified here, including: mesic flatwoods, sandhill, scrub, scrubby flatwoods, upland hardwood, mixed forests, xeric hammock, depression marsh, flood plain forest, swamp, hydric hammock and wet flatwoods. It is thus, a very diverse and excellent wildlife habitat. The most exotic wildlife species here are a clan of rhesus monkeys that live in the trees along the water's edge. These originally arrived as escapees from a local research facility but have since learned to thrive on their own. Some have contracted a monkey form of the AIDS virus but this is supposedly not transmittable to humans.

Et cetera: Size: 5000 acres. Marion County. Hours: sunrise to sunset. The museum is open to the public on weekends and holidays from 9:00 AM until 5:00 PM. Park entrance fee required. Camping available in beautiful new sites. Rental cabins and a picnic area will be added soon. Located inside the park is the Silver River Museum and Environmental Education Center. Head to the museum to learn about the park's rich cultural and natural history. From Paleo Indian occupation over 10,000 years ago to 1800's stage coach stops. Other activities include hiking, swimming, snorkeling, camping, nature study, etc.

When to Go: Because most of the trails are shaded, they can be enjoyed all year long.

Contacts: Silver River State Park, 1425 NE 58th Ave., Ocala, FL 34470; Phone (352) 236-7148

Directions: From Ocala on SR-40, head east to CR-35 (NE 58th Ave.). This juncture is in Silver Springs. Turn right heading south. The second paved road to the left is the main park entrance.

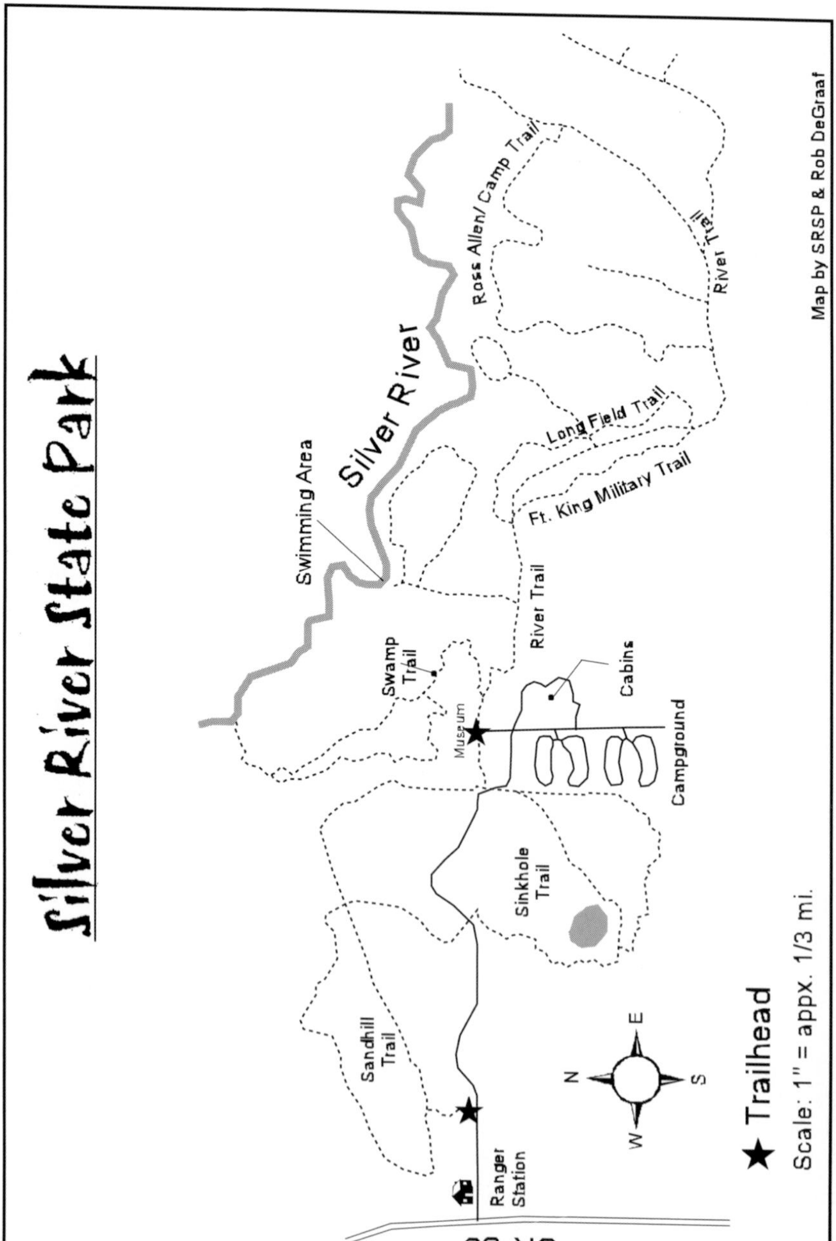

Silver River State Park
Silver River
Swimming Area
Swamp Trail
Museum
Cabins
Campground
River Trail
Ft. King Military Trail
Long Field Trail
Ross Allen/ Camp Trail
River Trail
Sinkhole Trail
Sandhill Trail
Ranger Station
SR-35
N
E
S
W
★ Trailhead
Scale: 1" = appx. 1/3 mi.
Map by SRSP & Rob DeGraaf

Ocklawaha Prairie Restoration Area

Location: Nearest town is Ocklawaha

Managing Agency: St. Johns River Water Management District (SJRWMD)

Trail Length: 12 miles

Difficulty: 40% beginner; 60% intermediate

Trail Type: 100% double track

Description: This is the place to see 100 years of humankind's so called progress in its perception and exploitation of the environment. Today, the diversity of natural systems provides habitat and feeding areas for a wide variety of wildlife. In the past, however, the course of the Ocklawaha River was altered to enhance the economic (agricultural) productivity of this rich bottom land. The entire prairie is encircled by a levee. Perched atop this levee is the trail. Viewing wildlife activity inside and outside of the prairie from here is excellent. Less than a mile from the trailhead, a high, pivoting, steel bridge with wooden planking crosses the Kyle Young Canal (known by the locals as the Ocklawaha Canal and frequently called the Ocklawaha River). Depending on rainfall to the south, this northerly flowing canal is often more than 20 feet below the top of the levee and the bridge. A viewing tower, perched on the levee's edge just south of the bridge, offers a great panoramic view of the prairie and is a great landmark as you pedal around the perimeter. The east and south sections of this trail offer a fairly smooth, very firm surface. This makes for enjoyable pedaling. The levee on the west side is not quite as high and while also fairly smooth and firm underneath, it has 8 or more inches of heavy grass which decreases your speed by about 50% for the same effort in a lower gear. Conditions in this section should improve in the cooler, drier months when grasses and other scrubby vegetation are at a minimum.

The eastern levee trail parallels the human-created Kyle Young Canal (C-212). Eventually the C-212 reconnects to the Ocklawaha River Channel at a small lake in the south. The "real" Ocklawaha River snakes throughout the mid-section of the prairie, and is accessible by canoe. It is a blackwater river, meaning that the tannins from the leaves of deciduous trees (those that loose their leaves seasonally) that fall into the river basin, decompose and give the slow flowing water a dark tea color. Before the C-212 canal was built in the early 1900's, this area was not wet at all. It was a gently sloping upland, vegetated mostly with pines, that led down to the low, broad flood plain along both banks of the river. The banks of the Ocklawaha River through this area were fairly indistinct. At times of high water, the river percolated through a system of small but interconnected freshwater marshes. Frequent flooding of these marshes left nutrient rich soils, providing a great resource for growing crops. Levees and ditches were built to drain much of the land and to control water flow. With gradual improvements in water control techniques, the flow in the historic Ocklawaha ceased completely by 1940. Talk about rich soil: in 1960 the manager of the local farm operations received an award from Iowa's DeKalb Corn

Company for the highest crop yield per unit seed of any other company operation.In 1991 SJRWMD purchased the Old Ocklawaha Farms property, now known as the Ocklawaha Prairie Restoration Area, to encourage the recovery of the native ecosystem which would in turn improve water quality on-site and expand flood storage area downstream.

<u>Wildlife:</u> A wide variety of wildlife species live in the area including: whitetail deer, black bear, bobcat, grey fox, alligator, gopher tortoise, sandhill crane, red tail hawk, sharp-shinned hawk, several species of sparrow, heron, egret and numerous waterfowl species. Butterflies, in great quantity and species diversity, flit throughout the prairie.

<u>Et cetera:</u> Size: 6,077 acres total. 2,400 acres of wetlands. Marion County. Hours: sunrise to sunset. Bring plenty of food and water (several bottles and/ or a hydration pack). A map and compass are recommended as is a first-aid kit; know how to use each. Also bring a couple of spare tubes, a pump, any vital tools, a lightweight raincoat, and insect repellent. The YMCA Refuge at Ocklawaha runs a retreat center on 52 acres of the property where the old homestead was. Included are 15 rustic cabins (some over 35 years old) sitting beneath enormous oak trees. The Refuge serves meals and offers open bus tours, canoe and horse rentals. 314 acre Chernobyl Memorial Forest in southern section of property contains longleaf pine uplands and honors those who lost their lives in the 1986 nuclear disaster in Ukraine. Nearby Marshal Swamp affords more off-road bicycling, as does the Ocala National Forest. See entries and locator map in this guide. Primitive camping, canoeing, hiking and horseback riding are other on site activities.

<u>When to Go:</u> Very little shade means one should ride at dawn or dusk in the summer, or during cooler months.

<u>Contacts:</u> St. Johns River Water Management District, Division of Land Management, PO Box 1429, Palatka, FL 32178, (800) 451-7106. On the web: www.sjr.state.fl.us ; For lodging and other Refuge activities call the YMCA Refuge: (352) 288-2233

<u>Directions:</u> From I-75, south of Ocala, take exit 341 east through Belleview. Starting as CR-484 this soon becomes Hwy 25 as it transverses Belleview. About 8 miles later, at the second blinking light in Ocklawaha, turn left on CR-464C (the "C" is important). In appx. 1.5 miles you'll see the first trailhead on the left. (Note: this author did not like the trails in southern area and suggests heading to northern trailhead instead). Continue on 464C for appx. 4 miles from Ocklawaha. Turn left on CR-314A. Just over a mile later 314A takes a right. Here you must instead head straight onto a dirt road (not well marked but it is Old River Road also called 137th Ave.). The trailhead is on your left in less than a mile. Note: A left off of CR-314A at the same intersection noted above leads to the YMCA Refuge at Ocklawaha.

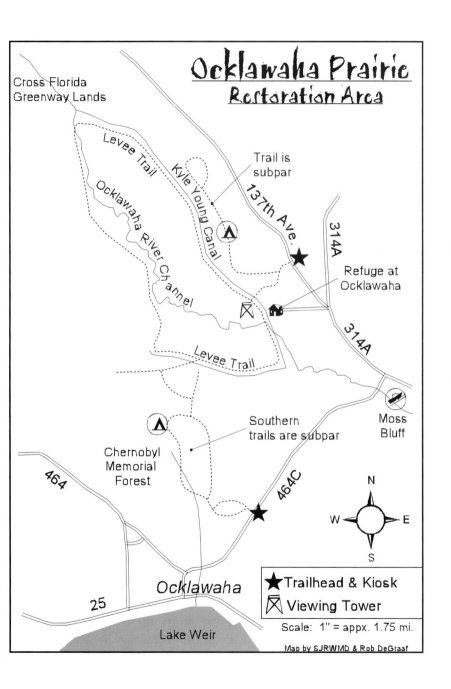

Ocklawaha Prairie
Restoration Area

Cross Florida
Greenway Lands

Levee Trail

Kyle Young Canal

Ocklawaha River Channel

Trail is
subpar

137th Ave.

314A

Refuge at
Ocklawaha

Levee Trail

314A

Southern
trails are subpar

Moss
Bluff

Chernobyl
Memorial
Forest

464

464C

N
W   E
S

Ocklawaha

25

Lake Weir

★ Trailhead & Kiosk
⊠ Viewing Tower

Scale: 1" = appx. 1.75 mi.

Map by SJRWMD & Rob DeGraaf

87

Sunnyhill Restoration Area

Location: Southwest of Ocala near Moss Bluff

Managing Agency: St. Johns River Water Management District

Trail Length: 24 miles

Difficulty: 100% intermediate

Trail Type: 100% doubletrack

Description: Located on the historic Ocklawaha River floodplain, this wetland restoration project trail follows the top of the canal levee on the west side while the trails on the east side are a combination of levees and other higher and drier elevated trails. For the most part, the western levee trail parallels the Ocklawaha Canal (C-231) providing great vistas to the east and west of the flower and bird filled marsh and of the dark water, cypress knees, flowers and wildlife along the canal. Five miles from the northern entrance of this levee trail is a bird watching shelter, complete with a blind and a (landmark from the other side) green roof. From the southern entrance (Blue House Information Center) it is 2.5 miles to this shelter. On the east side of the historic Ocklawaha River Channel and marsh there are two trails that closely parallel each other going north and south. The eastern most of these trails has bad sugar sand stretches, many bumps, and mucky sections after wet weather. Using the more western of these trails provides more enjoyable biking and offers better, more encompassing views. A large variety of wild flowers and butterflies thrive at trail side. About a mile directly north of the southern entrance is a covered observation tower. Directly east of this landmark is a significant hill with a radio tower on its top. This is Sunnyhill and it also makes for a good landmark. A trailhead and parking area are located here.

Overall, most of the trail surfaces are grass. The southern half of the property seems to experience more traffic, thus trails are better packed and are easier to ride. Riding from the northern most entrance on the east side (one mile south of CR-314A), the cyclist is required to ford a stream almost immediately. Depth varies depending on rainfall but wading is necessary. Trail access and parking one mile further south (on FR-8) avoids the necessity of getting your feet wet or having to remove your shoes early in the ride. Also, primitive camping is permitted near this latter entrance (see map).

Wildlife: A wide variety of wading birds feed in the marshes along the trail. Red-tailed and red-shouldered hawk, osprey and three owl species live here year-round. Sandhill cranes spend the winter here. Vultures circling overhead are waiting to see how often you take a drink. If you drink often, they will fly on. If not, well. . . . The size of these mosquitoes might lead you to think that they too are birds. Black bear, river otter, bobcat, whitetail deer and other wildlife are returning to the area as restoration proceeds.

Et cetera: Size: 4,357 acres. Marion County. Hours: sunrise to sunset. An old farmhouse on the property, known as the Blue House, showcases an exhibit of the Ocklawaha River Basin as it has changed over time. The house is open on Sunday from 1-4 PM or for group tours by appointment. Load up on drinking water and mosquito repellent. Bring a light snack. Other activities include: hiking, nature study, fishing, horseback riding, paddling, boating and camping.

When to Go: Because there is little shade along most of the trails, it's advised to ride dawn or dusk during the summer or anytime during cooler months.

Contacts: St. Johns River Water Management District, Division of Land Management, PO Box 1429, Palatka, FL 32178, (800) 451-7106. On the web: www.sjr.state.fl.us

Directions: The southern entrance is on the north side of SR-42, 5.9 miles east of Weirsdale. Make an immediate left just after crossing the bridge over the Ocklawaha River. 1.5 miles further west on SR-42, taking a left (heading north) on SE 182 Avenue Road, leads to numerous other trailheads on the left side of road (see map). To access the northern entrance to the western levee trail, proceed south on 464C from 314A at Moss Bluff for .2 miles. Before crossing the river bridge, turn left into the boat launch area.

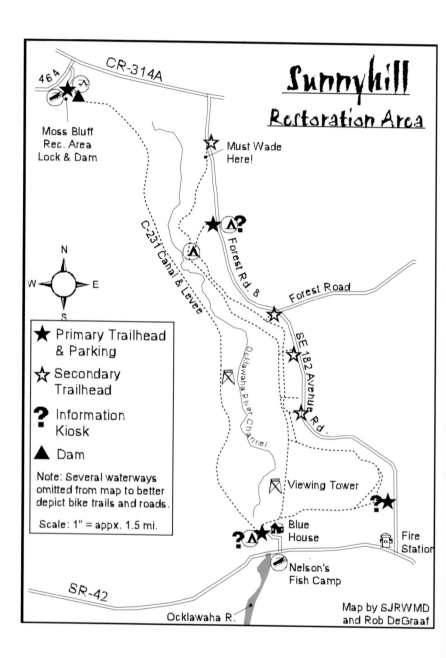

Sunnyhill
Restoration Area

CR-314A

464

Moss Bluff
Rec. Area
Lock & Dam

Must Wade
Here!

C-231 Canal & Levee

Forest Rd. 8

Forest Road

SE 182 Avenue Rd.

Ocklawaha River Channel

Primary Trailhead
& Parking

Secondary
Trailhead

? Information
Kiosk

▲ Dam

Note: Several waterways
omitted from map to better
depict bike trails and roads.

Scale: 1" = appx. 1.5 mi.

Viewing Tower

Blue
House

Fire
Station

Nelson's
Fish Camp

SR-42

Ocklawaha R.

Map by SJRWMD
and Rob DeGraaf

N
W   E
S

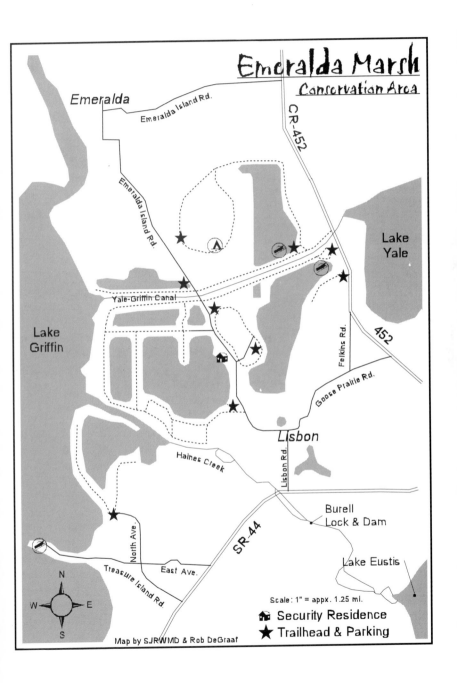

Emeralda Marsh
Conservation Area

Emeralda

Emeralda Island Rd.

CR-452

Emeralda Island Rd.

Lake Yale

Yale-Griffin Canal

Lake Griffin

Felkins Rd.

452

Goose Prairie Rd.

Lisbon

Haines Creek

Lisbon Rd.

Burell Lock & Dam

SR-44

Lake Eustis

North Ave.

East Ave.

Treasure Island Rd.

Scale: 1" = appx. 1.25 mi.

🏠 Security Residence
★ Trailhead & Parking

N
W   E
S

Map by SJRWMD & Rob DeGraaf

91

Emeralda Marsh Conservation Area

Location: 12 miles northeast of Leesburg

Managing Agency: St. Johns River Water Management District

Trail Length: 24 miles

Difficulty: 30% beginner; 70% intermediate

Trail Type: 100% doubletrack

Description: Do you want to see birds, birds and more birds? This is certainly the place to do that. Yes, you will probably see alligators and other wildlife, but it is the winged ones that reign supreme here. Most of the population consists of waterfowl and migrating birds.

The easiest riding as well as the best birding are available by entering in the west from Emeralda Island Road, about 2 miles north of the town of Lisbon. This entrance is about half a mile south of the canal that passes between Lake Griffin and Lake Yale and crosses under Emeralda Island Rd. There is no gate preventing vehicles from entering here and automobiles can continue a mile down this hard pack, lime rock road. However, don't drive this portion and risk losing the great ride and views. Instead, park just off of the Emeralda Island Road and bike in.

A large variety of wading birds can be seen on both sides of the trail, which at this point is only a few inches above the water level. The trail continues west for a total of 1.7 miles with several trails off to the north and south. Most of this is comfortable riding for beginners. A little map reading and some planning can provide several loop trails. For the stronger or more dedicated rider, the trails along the tops of the levees provide great views but require a bit more effort as they are typically overgrown with grass. Below the friction causing grass, the trails have a firm surface. Rudy saw more than 50 great blue herons here in a single day. On one bush, alone, he saw 11 double-crested cormorants. The birds appear accustomed to human traffic and are less skittish than in most other locations. Trail sections along the south edge of main marsh provide the best shade.

Wildlife: A large number of the eastern greater sandhill crane population winters in the area. Thousands of ring-necked ducks and lesser numbers of wood ducks, Florida ducks, hooded mergansers as well as large flocks of white pelicans and other water fowl species can be seen in the area. Rare and endangered species include bald eagle, wood stork, limpkin and snowy egret. Even red-winged black birds are plentiful. The wetlands and adjacent water bodies support one of the highest alligator populations in central Florida, therefore keep alert. Whitetail deer, rabbit and other common mammals are present.

Et cetera: Size: 7,089 acres. Lake and Marion Counties. Hours: sunrise to sunset. Suggested items to bring include: sun screen, insect repellent, plenty of water and food. A bird identification book makes a nice addition on wetland/ raised levee trails like Emeralda. Hunting is permitted here in season. Call for dates before heading out.

When to Go: Go early in the morning or near sunset during the hot summer months or any time from September through April. Avoid riding during waterfowl hunting season.

Contacts: St. Johns River Water Management District, Division of Land Management, PO Box 1429, Palatka, FL 32178, (800) 451-7106. On the web: www.sjr.state.fl.us

Directions: From the north travel east from Weirsdale on SR-42 passing the Sunnyhill Restoration Area. Turn south on CR-452. Turn right on Emeralda Island Road and follow this through numerous sharp turns for about 4.5 miles. Turn right onto the white, lime rock road heading into the marsh. Park here. There are numerous entrances both north and south of here on this road. There are also entrances off of CR-452 north and south of the Yale-Griffin Canal. The southern most entrance is off of SR-44, south of Lisbon. From SR-44, take Treasure Island Road north. Continue heading north through intersection. Road then becomes North Treasure Island Ave. There is parking and a trailhead at the end of this road.

Lake Panasoffkee Wildlife Management Area

Location: 12 miles east of Inverness

Managing Agency: Southwest Florida Water Management District (SWFWMD) and Florida Fish and Wildlife Conservation Commission (FF&WCC)

Trail Length: 12.7 miles

Difficulty: 100% intermediate

Trail Type: 100% doubletrack

Description: Peaceful, quiet and beautiful are just a few adjectives that describe the Lake Panasoffkee Project (formerly known as the Hanover Tract). Towering grandfather oaks and magnificent magnolias stand as elegant silhouettes while you pass beneath their shade. Grassy meadows seem to stretch endlessly beneath the trees in all directions. The doubletrack trail itself is covered with grass except along the very heavily shaded berms through the swamps. While riding through grass generally slows progress, here it holds together sand that tends to be unridable where grass is lacking.

From the parking area it is best to immediately ride west. Heading directly south on the loop leads to quick discouragement as there are some very sandy sections here. Equestrian traffic keeps these soft sections a nightmare for cyclists. By heading west one bypasses the soft stuff and still eventually continues south onto the Jones Creek Trail. The end of the Borrow Pit Trail near I-75, due to long sugar sand stretches, should also be avoided unless you don't mind dismounting and pushing.

Lake Pan (for short) is a favorite venue for equestrians who are generally very friendly and helpful. For the most part, it is they who maintain these trails through "The Friends of Hanover," a locally active volunteer group. Please exercise trail etiquette and avoid spooking horses when approaching to insure continued cooperation between trail users. Yield trail to equestrian users. Do so by dismounting from your bicycle and advancing a friendly greeting. Also, maintaining a calm dialogue as horses pass impresses riders and relaxes horses.

The property lies along the eastern shore of Lake Panasoffkee. It was acquired between 1990 and 1997 to preserve the lake's vast flood plain forest. Also protected are the pine flatwoods, freshwater marshes and oak scrub forest. The flood plain forest protects water resources by cleansing rain runoff before it enters the lake or seeps into the ground and by naturally holding back storm water that could cause flooding. Spring fed, Little Jones and Big Jones Creeks meander through the forest before emptying into the northern section of the lake. After heavy rainfall, Little Jones Creek rushes under a trail bridge. This is a great place to relax, grab a snack and take wilderness photos.

Wildlife: Most wildlife are observed by quiet riders near dawn and dusk. This is also the best time to listen to owls hooting. During the warmer months, mosquitoes seem to schedule their main meals near the hours when the sun is near the horizon.

Whitetail deer, armadillo, feral hog, raccoon, turkey, hawks, vultures, meadowlarks and sparrows frequent trail side areas. The ponds and creeks are excellent for viewing turtles, frogs, various fish and wading birds.

Et cetera: Size: 9,911 acres. Sumter County. Hours: sunrise to sunset. Bring plenty of food and water (several bottles and/ or a hydration pack). A map and compass are recommended as is a first-aid kit; know how to use each. Also bring a couple of spare tubes, a pump, any vital tools, a lightweight rain-coat and insect repellent. Hunting permitted in season. Call for dates before heading out.

When to Go: Riding here is pleasant year round as much of the trail is shaded. Open areas can be very hot mid-summer. The sandy sections are much easier to ride after rainfall since sand gets better as it gets wetter.

Contacts: Southwest Florida Water Management District, Land Resources Department, 2379 Broad St., Brooksville, FL 34604, (800) 423-1476 ext. 4470. On the web: www.swfwmd.state.fl.us ; Florida Fish & Wildlife Conservation Commission, 620 S. Meridian St., Tallahassee, FL 32399, (850) 488-4676 or (352) 732-1225. On the web: www.state.fl.us/fwc

Directions: From the east: from I-75 take exit #329 and head west on SR-44 for appx. 4 miles. Watch for an entrance sign and dirt entrance road on the left. From the west: in Inverness, take SR-44 east from US-41 for about 12.5 miles. The entrance sign and dirt entrance road are on your right. Park in the grass under the trees. Remember, to avoid soft sand, bike west from here!

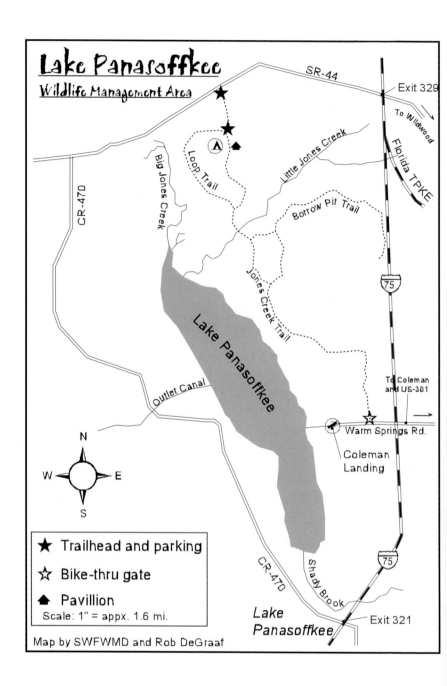

Lake Panasoffkee
Wildlife Management Area

SR-44
Exit 329
To Wildwood
Florida TPKE
CR-470
Big Jones Creek
Loop Trail
Little Jones Creek
Borrow Pit Trail
I-75
Jones Creek Trail
Lake Panasoffkee
Outlet Canal
To Coleman and US-301
Warm Springs Rd.
Coleman Landing
N
W E
S

★ Trailhead and parking

☆ Bike-thru gate

♠ Pavillion

Scale: 1" = appx. 1.6 mi.

CR-470
Shady Brook
I-75
Lake Panasoffkee
Exit 321

Map by SWFWMD and Rob DeGraaf

Potts Preserve Wildlife Management Area

Location: Northeast of Inverness

Managing Agency: Southwest Florida Water Management District (SWFWMD) and Florida Fish and Wildlife Conservation Commission (FF&WCC)

Trail Length: 27 miles

Difficulty: 20% beginner; 60% intermediate; 20% advanced

Trail Type: 100% doubletrack

Description: Have you ever been in a small airplane flying over a beautiful, desolate, Florida ranch with jeep trails emerging from one wooded area only to disappear into another, and wished you could ride your bike there? If so, this is the place to realize your dreams. Located on the western banks of the black, tannic waters of the Withlacoochee River, Potts Preserve reaches about 4 miles west into the waters and wetlands of Tsala Apopka Lake. Beautiful cypress trees with stalagmite knees and arms draped in Spanish moss guard the river corridor from both of its banks. From the eastern entry point on Hooty Point Road the trail heading north opens into an expansive pasture spotted with magnificent, huge grandfather oaks whose limbs are covered with resurrection fern. The openness of the views towards the river are more picturesque than what is usually found along the heavily wooded river banks. As the trails wind further north and west they are thickly canopied through oak hammocks and flatwoods terrain. An exception is the George Washington Pasture in the northeast (see map) which is mostly open grassland with scrub oak communities on its edges. Aside from these uplands, most of the Preserve is wet, especially in the western half. For you, this is an undiscovered gem as records indicate only 430 visitors in the year 2000.

Trails leaving from both main trailheads offer a very hard surface for the first mile. These conditions offer excellent family and beginner riding. Trails heading through the marshes in the west follow old dikes. This region is designated for equestrian use (which appears almost non-existent) and provides the only hunters entrance. Hunting vehicles and the lack of shade have left some sugar sand stretches that require great strength and determination to ride. Don't forget, however, that walking the tough sections soon puts you where others are less willing to go. Trails leaving from the eastern entrance offer many miles of beginner to intermediate riding on firm, shaded surfaces. Some of the most northern trails also offer firm surfaces and shade while the perimeter of the George Washington Pasture offers little shade and a soft riding surface.

Before it was publically acquired, between 1988 -1993, this land was known as the Dee River Ranch. This former ranch is large and isolated. Isolated, in that it is almost completely surrounded by wetlands, lakes or the Withlacoochee River. The preserve is named after Michael T. Potts, a SWFWMD employee who died here in an accident while working on a pre-acquisition land survey.

A warning in advance: overall, the trails here are poorly marked. Equestrian signs denote 12 miles for horseback riding. Hikers have 16 miles of orange blazed main trail and 4 miles of blue blazed side trails including the river trail. Often, the hiking trails parallel doubletrack trails open to cyclists.

<u>Wildlife:</u> Deer, wild turkey, Eastern blue bird, meadow birds and wading birds are common. Also present are fox squirrel, gopher tortoise, armadillo, raccoon, opossum and a few threatened Florida scrub jays. There are both wetland and upland habitats here including freshwater marsh, floodplain forest, scrub oak, flatwoods and oak hammocks. The marsh areas include numerous types of grasses, swamp lilies and blue flag irises.

<u>Et cetera:</u> Size: 9,349 acres. Citrus County. Hours: sunrise to sunset. Remember that much of this preserve is wet, so bringing mosquito repellent is a wise idea. Even with a compass and a good map it is often difficult to pinpoint your location here, so be cautious. Be sure to bring plenty of drinking water and be prepared to fix normal mechanical failures and flat tires as walking out is probably your only other option. Anticipate wet spots and water crossings. Primitive camping by permit is allowed in several areas with no vehicle access. Canoe camping by permit is also allowed along the river. Be sure to obtain a hunt schedule and avoid riding on those dates. One of the only negatives about Potts is that the peace and quiet of this beautiful wilderness is sometimes interrupted by loud air boats which can be heard more than half a mile away. This is much less often the case on weekdays.

<u>When to Go:</u> Make your first visit during the cool months or early in the morning. Once you know your way around, come back and ride on warm or rainy days.

<u>Contacts:</u> Southwest Florida Water Management District, Land Resources Department, 2379 Broad Street, Brooksville, FL 34604, (800) 423-1476 x. 4470. On the web: www.swfwmd.state.fl.us ; Florida Fish & Wildlife Conservation Commission, 620 S. Meridian St., Tallahassee, FL 32399, (850) 488-4676. On the web: www.state.fl.us/fwc

<u>Directions:</u> The only two trailheads into the property are off of CR-581, which dead-ends after heading northeast out of Inverness. From the junction of SR-44 and US-41, just west of downtown Inverness, take US-41 north. Drive appx. two blocks before CR-581 turns to the right, heading east. Then drive a few blocks before turning left, heading north. Five miles of winding road from here leads to Dee River Rd. on your left. Follow the Potts Preserve sign to the western trailhead. To reach the eastern trailhead, stay on CR-581, and continue heading northeast past Dee River Rd. Drive appx. 1.2 miles, then turn left onto Hooty Point Rd. The trailhead is on your left in .2 miles.

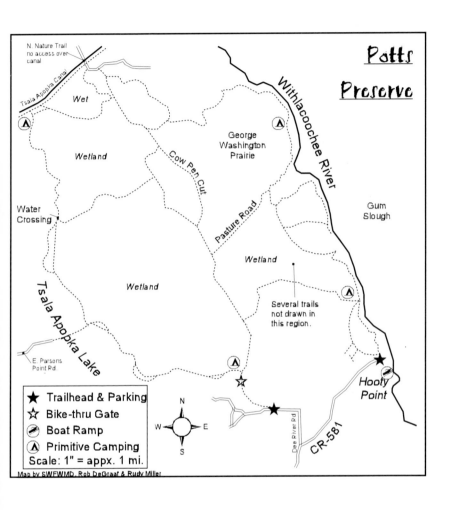

Potts Preserve

N. Nature Trail
no access over
canal

Tsala Apopka Canal

Wet

Wetland

Withlacoochee River

George
Washington
Prairie

Cow Pen Cut

Pasture Road

Gum
Slough

Water
Crossing

Wetland

Wetland

Several trails
not drawn in
this region.

Tsala Apopka Lake

E. Parsons
Point Rd.

Hooty
Point

★ Trailhead & Parking
☆ Bike-thru Gate
⊘ Boat Ramp
Ⓐ Primitive Camping
Scale: 1" = appx. 1 mi.

N
W   E
S

Dee River Rd

CR-581

Map by SWFWMD, Rob DeGraaf & Rudy Miller

99

Gum Slough / Half-Moon
Wildlife Management Areas

Location: Nearest towns: Rutland and Inverness

Managing Agency: Florida Fish and Wildlife Conservation Commission and Southwest Florida Water Management District

Trail Length: 16 miles

Difficulty: 90% beginner; 10% intermediate

Trail Type: 100% doubletrack

Description: These two tracts of land share a common boundary in the middle, with Gum Slough on the west and Half-Moon to the east. Trails run back and forth through both properties without informing the cyclist as to which property he or she is in. Only a few of these trails are gated at the boundaries, however, these are unlocked, walk/ bike through gates (see map).

Riding a bike through Half-Moon WMA is much like riding through a Florida ranch with smooth hard packed, double track roads. The terrain is flat and open with green pastures running beneath the oaks and pines. Bicycling is allowed on the designated or marked, shared-use trails. Most of the time, the many cattle seem more afraid of the rider than the other way around, but when 30 curious cows all come toward you at once remember to leave them alone as this is the preference of their owner.

Mill Creek Road, the main north-south corridor on Half-Moon, is great for family and group rides but the road itself has little shade. Spurs from here reach deeper into the well canopied woods. The condition of these roads deteriorates the further one rides in.

At eight tenths of a mile from the parking area, Wall Road goes left and enters Gum Slough. Appx. 1.2 miles later this trail makes a sharp right up onto an abandoned tram road. This is real back-country as this western edge track is rarely visited. This also implies that there isn't much of a trail, and many downed logs and spider webs may be encountered. This trail heads mostly north as it parallels the hidden-from-view, Withlacoochee River to the west. Spur roads heading east from the tram road will lead back to Mill Creek Road (see map).

In July 2001 one of the authors, while traveling this route, noted "wave" activity in a small, almost dry mud hole. Curious, he stood high on the bank and used a 20 foot pole to poke into the mud. Suddenly, a 7-foot long, agitated alligator emerged and grabbed at the pole. In the best interests of not harassing wildlife and of protecting himself, the author left, taking with him a great memory and a more cautious view toward mud puddles.

<u>Wildlife:</u> Feral hog, whitetail deer, fox squirrel, coyote, river otter, bobcat, armadillo, ubiquitous cattle and alligator in the wetter regions. Birds include wild turkey, great horned owl, Eastern screech owl, Eastern bluebird, swallow-tailed kite, red-shouldered hawk, red-headed woodpecker, anhinga, limpkin, sand-hill crane, etc.

<u>Et cetera:</u> Size: Gum Slough = 4,104 acres. Half Moon = 9,480 acres. Marion and Sumter Counties. Hours are sunrise to sunset. Note: Gum Slough is also called the "Carlton Tract." Some of the less traveled and less maintained roads are not noted on this map. No camping. Bring plenty of food and water (several bottles and/ or a hydration pack). A map, compass and GPS are recommended as is a first-aid kit; know how to use each. Also bring a couple of spare tubes, a pump and any vital tools. Insect repellent, sun screen, and rain gear also suggested. This is a wild area encompassing thousands of acres so be prepared. Weekend hunting in late October and November prohibits biking. Call 1-800-955-8771 to obtain hunt dates.

<u>When to Go:</u> Fall, winter and spring are the most enjoyable seasons to bike here, as they are cooler. During hot weather, dawn or dusk rides are advised. Call for hunt dates before heading out.

<u>Contacts:</u> Florida Fish & Wildlife Conservation Commission, 620 S. Meridian St., Tallahassee, FL 32399,

Mighk Wilson and others on a Gum Slough group ride
Photo by Rob DeGraaf

(850) 488-4676. On the web: www.state.fl.us/fwc; Southwest Florida Water Management District, Land Resources Department, 2379 Broad St., Brooksville, FL 34604, (800) 423-1476 ext. 4470. On the web: www.swfwmd.state.fl.us

<u>Directions:</u> From Inverness at US Hwy. 41 take FL Hwy. 44 East 7.7 miles to CR 247. From I-75 take exit # 329 West on SR-44 for 7.5 miles to CR-247. Here there is a small sign pointing north that says "Half-Moon WMA" on both sides of it and a small green street sign with "CR-247" on it. Across the street to the south is the First Baptist Church of Rutland. Take CR-247 North 1.5 miles to the parking area and entrance.

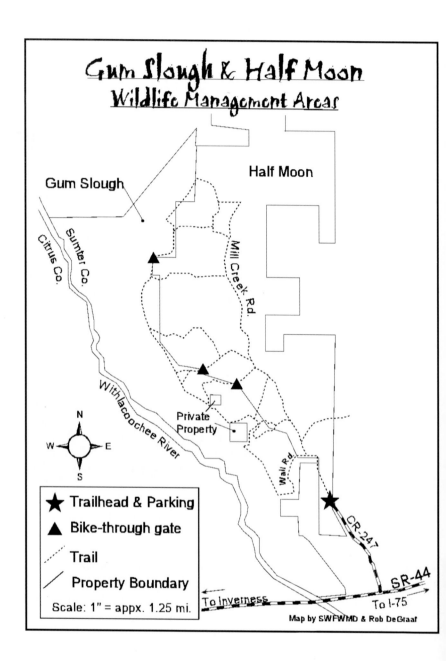

Gum Slough & Half Moon
Wildlife Management Areas

Half Moon

Gum Slough

Citrus Co.

Sumter Co.

Mill Creek Rd.

Withlacoochee River

Private Property

Wall Rd.

N
W   E
S

★ Trailhead & Parking
▲ Bike-through gate
Trail
Property Boundary
Scale: 1" = appx. 1.25 mi.

CR-247

SR-44

To Inverness

To I-75

Map by SWFWMD & Rob DeGraaf

Withlacoochee State Forest - Homosassa Tract and Homosassa Wildlife Management Area

Location: South of Homosassa Springs

Managing Agency: Florida Division of Forestry, Florida Fish and Wildlife Conservation Commission and the Southwest Florida Water Management District.

Trail Length: 22 miles

Difficulty: Depends on speed and length of stay

Trail Type: 100% doubletrack

Description: We decided that the Homosassa property deserved a full writeup and trail map due to its overall quality for off-road bicycling. In some respects, Homosassa is assembled like a jigsaw puzzle: some sections are managed by Fish and Wildlife, some by Division of Forestry and still others by the Water Management District. Finding one map covering, accurately, the system of trails on all three agencies' lands proved to be impossible. We therefore combined several separate maps to produce the one provided here.

Homosassa is well suited to riders who seek a beautiful, varied, wilderness experience. There are many trail loops of various lengths. Large loops both north and south of Burnt Bridge Road are about 9 miles each and many shorter options are in the northern half of the property. All of the terrain is fairly level with the doubletrack being hard packed lime rock or otherwise quite firm with a thin grass covering. Immediately west of the main parking area is an old group of clear, sheer walled, lime rock pits that are beautiful and peaceful. The trail into these has some rare sandy patches. Similar lakes in old mining pits are found in the Hog Pond area north of Mason Creek (see map).

Elevated, old logging trails throughout the hardwood swamp, with their arching tree limbs shading the trail, lie in sharp contrast to the open pasture areas dotted with small islands of oak trees. Various maturities of planted long leaf pines are scattered throughout the property, much of which was pasture before it was purchased through Florida's Conservation and Recreation Lands Program in the early 90's.

From the main trailhead, on Burnt Bridge Rd., biking one mile northwest leads to a narrow bridge. This crosses Mason Creek (also known as Hidden River). The clear flowing water comes from a few small springs to the east, upstream. Downstream, the creek enters a small pond then, strangely, vanishes underground without flowing into the Gulf of Mexico as do most spring-fed creeks in the area. It is thought that the system re-enters the aquifer at this point but its course of action beyond this is unknown. One of the authors is fortunate enough to visit here regularly for work to sample the springs for water quality.

Designated trailheads with parking are shown on the map. There are other public access points into the property, however, these typically do not have parking and some are prone to vandalism. They are useful to know about in case an alternate exit point is needed either in time of emergency, to restock supplies (e.g., water and food), or just for a change of pace. Trails leading to these access points are enjoyable and scenic, therefore, should be included in your ride if time permits. There are locked gates at these points to prevent motorized vehicles from illegally entering the property. Bikes can be ridden around or passed over the gates fairly easily. In the south, trail-3 runs into trail-2 (called W. Lykes Trail off Forest property). It is extremely scenic and well canopied, west of the trail-2 and trail-3 intersection (see map). In the other direction, W. Lykes Trail heads south to SR-480. . . . In the north, BOB Road leads to a gate then exits onto Central St. in residential Homosassa. Continuing straight will lead into town. . . . Heading south from town on S. Chamberlain Pool Ave. leads to a gated access point, scenic yet troubled with vandalism at the same time. The trail tees at Otter Creek. Overgrown brush to the west thwarts much exploration in that direction, while more open trail leads to the east, paralleling scenic, spring fed Otter Creek. This trail leads to trails 11 and 12. Trail 12 is a superb out-and-back paralleling Otter Creek on the south side. 11 seems to peter out in the south and leads to another gate in the north, at Woodland Pl. which runs back into Chamberlain Pool Ave. in Homosassa. We were unable to link these woods trails back to others without backtracking thru town first.

<u>Wildlife:</u> Black bear, deer, wild hog, wild turkey, raccoon, armadillo, fox squirrel, hawk, owl, sandhill crane, osprey, occasional bald eagle, great blue heron, and many others are found here. The tract is ecologically diverse boasting eleven different natural communities. Included are bottomland forest, swamp, blackwater streams, flatwoods, pine forest and scrub. You can observe the changes between these communities by noting their physical characteristics and unique plants. The area includes most of the vegetation species that naturally occur in central Florida.

<u>Et cetera:</u> Size: 11,143 acres. Citrus County. Hours: 5:00 a.m. to 8:00 p.m. Bring plenty of food and water (several bottles and/ or a hydration pack). A map and compass are recommended as is a first-aid kit; know how to use each. Also bring a couple of spare tubes, a pump, any vital tools, a lightweight rain-coat, and insect repellent. This is a wild area encompassing thousands of acres. . . . A bird observation trail is expected to open in Homosassa in 2002.

<u>When to Go:</u> Anytime other than during scheduled hunts.

<u>Contacts:</u> Withlacoochee State Forest Recreation/Visitor Center, 15003 Broad St., Brooksville, FL 34601, (352) 754-6896. On the web: www.fl-dof.com ; Florida Fish & Wildlife Conservation Commission, 620 S. Meridian St., Tallahassee, FL 32399, (850) 488-4676. On the web: www.state.fl.us/fwc

<u>Directions:</u> Located 5 ½ miles south of Homosassa Springs. At the intersection of US-98 and US-19, drive north 1.6 miles to the fire tower (across from Sugar Mill Woods) and turn left. Appx. 1.8 miles ahead on Burnt Bridge Road is the main parking area with other parking opportunities along the way. There is also a northern trailhead/ parking area 3.3 miles north of the fire tower on the west side of US-19.

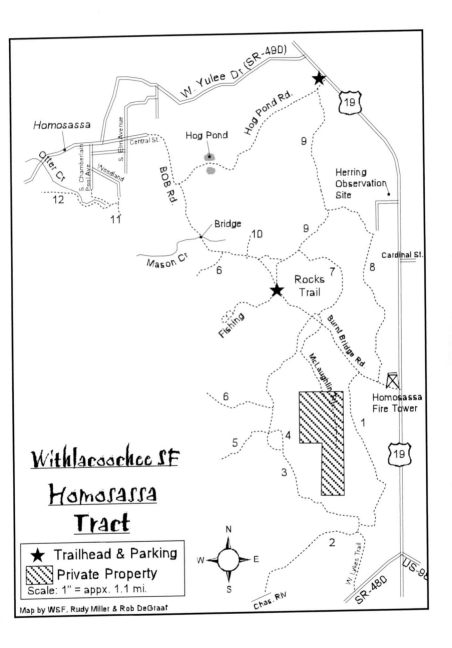

Withlacoochee SF
Homosassa
Tract

★ Trailhead & Parking
░ Private Property
Scale: 1" = appx. 1.1 mi.

Map by WSF, Rudy Miller & Rob DeGraaf

Withlacoochee State Forest

Location: See each tract for nearest towns.

Managing Agency: Florida Department of Agriculture and Consumer Services, Division of Forestry

Trail Length: See separate listings

Difficulty: Depends on speed and length of stay

Trail Type: 100% doubletrack

Description: The Withlacoochee State Forest is absolutely huge. Over 155,000 acres are divided into a half dozen or so separate tracts, some of these being quite distant from one another. Fortunately, most permit off-road bicycling. The Croom Tract has the only singletrack in the group. It also has doubletrack. The other tracts afford plenty of scenic and uncrowded doubletrack riding. Many of these properties offer primitive camping and most allow hunting in season, which runs throughout the winter months. Call contact numbers below to obtain hunt dates (to avoid) and camping information.

Baird Tract

This is a great place to take a wilderness ride! 16.8 miles of mostly hardpack, doubletrack roads cross wild and scenic terrain. This is remote land where humans are a rare species, except during hunting season (call for dates). There are four major out and back side trails from the main loop, each near a mile in length. Revel Road leads north under a beautifully shaded arch of limbs, however, this shade doesn't last long as much of the trail offers little shade. In the fall, myriad shades of yellow flowering plants sway in the sun, spreading bright yellow waves along the trail. A couple of these are: Black-eyed Susan and several varieties of goldenrod .

The quiet rider will likely see wild turkey, white tailed deer and near dusk, bobcat. Other wildlife includes gopher tortoise, hawk, raccoon, armadillo, opossum, gray squirrel, rabbit, etc. Bicycles may be operated only on named or numbered roads and designated fire lanes. Motor vehicles are prohibited except during scheduled hunts which run from late September to late March. Important note: there are many days during this cooler/ drier season when there are no scheduled hunts so call in advance or check the schedule (for your safety and solitude). Be sure to bring insect repellent, plenty of water, a trail snack, pump, tubes, tools, first aid kit, etc.

Located 18 miles west of Clermont in Sumter County. The 11,576 acres of the Baird Tract abuts the James A. Van Fleet State Rail Trail. The Van Fleet is an exceptional, isolated and scenic, rail trail. From SR-50 in Tarrytown at CR-471, go south 1.9 miles to the main entrance on your left. Riders can also enter from the Van Fleet State Trail at the gate about 1.7 miles south of the SR-50 (Van Fleet) trailhead. This trailhead is about 5 miles east of Tarrytown and the CR-471 junction.

Citrus Tract

More than 100 miles of doubletrack roads can be found here. The difficulty split is appx. 30% beginner; 60% intermediate; 10% advanced. This section of State Forest covers 41,000 acres in Citrus and Hernando Counties. Trails are shared with vehicles, most of this to be found on TR13. The eleven miles of hard packed surface of TR13 makes it the easiest to ride. It is also the central access to the east-west trails. This tract consists of rolling hills with a clay or sand base and a variety of plant communities. Rain tends to gather in low lying areas. Difficult sandy sections to avoid include TR17 between TR2 and TR6, TR11 between TR2 and TR16, and TR22 from TR15 to TR13. Excellent sections in the NW include TR19 from TR10A to TR2. Note: only a small percentage of roads offer shade, so early morning or October through April riding is best. Avoid hunting season from mid-November through mid-March.

There are 6 cave entrances in the SW area. To find these, take SR-98 NW from Brooksville turning right onto CR-491. Take this .8 miles past the intersection of CR-480 and park along the highway opposite W. Lone Ct. road to the west. Bike .6 miles east on the main trail (it all keeps joining back together) to an open area on your right with a small cable fence. Beyond the fence and also to your left are 5 cave openings, two of which connect underground and have further caves from there. Local spelunkers slide in and out of these caves when the weather has been fairly dry. This can be fun, but make sure to have at least two flashlights, at least two persons and wear your bike helmets. .2 miles further east on the same trail is the 6th cave on your right. At one mile from your car the Citrus Hiking Trail crosses TR22 which you are on. The northern portion of this hiking trail is most beautiful but bikers are excluded. If you turn left at 1.2 miles from your car (just beyond the hiking trail) you will be on TR15. Great riding for skilled riders is on TR14 between TR15 and TR13. There is significant elevation change here and erosion has left some clay ruts bigger than cars. Advanced riders will also find some of the sandy sections a test of their skills and strength.

Full hookup, fee camping is available at Tillis Hill off of TR13 just north of TR20, with other good camping at Mutual Mine and at Holder Mine.

Abundant wildlife including: deer, feral hog, gray squirrel, rabbit, raccoon, gopher tortoise, opossum, armadillo, coyote, skunk, bobcat and mink. Migratory game birds and quail may also be seen. Potable water is available at all three camping areas. Carrying a map and a compass will help you stay oriented. Check for hunt dates.

Located NW of Brooksville. The most northern entrance is TR13 which is south of SR44 and about 5 miles west of Inverness. There are two entrances off of CR-581 which runs north (left turn) off of US-41, north of Brooksville. CR-581 continues to SR-44 west of Inverness. Note signs for Mutual Mine and Holder Mine on CR-581. CR-480 runs east and west between CR-581. CR-491 and the southern entrance to TR13 is between these.

Croom Tract

See separate listing under "Singletrack Rides." Note the many miles of doubletrack as well as singletrack here.

Homosassa Tract

See separate listing and map in this section.

Richloam Tract

Located appx. 20 miles east of Brooksville, Richloam weighs in at 56,400 acres, and boasts over 200 miles of trail. Just think, this is just one tract in the state forest! Lands this large offer up plenty of adventure at the same time they afford heightened risks of getting very lost. Improved dirt roads offer even the novice rider an opportunity to explore the back country, but the unimproved roads offer a more adventuresome spirit unique challenges and almost limitless solitude. These untamed roads crisscross the property and include numerous wet sections here and there. Some of these can be skirted while others cannot. Snakes and alligators make their homes here so be cautious riding into unknown waters, especially during the gator spring mating season when males move considerable distances and tend to be testy. In dry seasons there will be some sandy sections. Although all the trails are hardpack sand, the frequent large mud puddles keep out almost all motor vehicles. This usually allows you to enjoy the beauty of this wilderness alone or with just your group. While not as wet as the Green Swamp, adjacent to the south, there is more water than dry land here during rainy season. With a few exceptions, the improved roads are usually above water.

Animals that you may see include deer, feral hog, racoon, bobcat, opossum, skunk, rabbit and armadillo. Wild turkey, hawk, owl, and vulture are commonly sited while bald eagle are spotted occasionally. Plant communities include pine flatwoods, cypress domes and hardwood hammocks to name just a few.

Call for hunt dates before heading out! Primitive campsites are available but check first on conditions regarding their use. Bring plenty of water (several bottles and/ or a hydration pack), food, insect repellant and sun screen, and use each frequently. Dehydration can occur rapidly in the summer. A map, compass and GPS (if available) are recommended as is a first-aid kit; know how to use each. Also bring a couple of spare tubes, a pump and any vital tools. This is a wild area encompassing thousands of acres so be prepared. Bicycles not permitted on hiking trails.

Best to avoid overly hot, summer days or periods following prolonged rains or dry spells. There are wonderful gaps in the winter hunting season when you can really enjoy this area. If you are an early riser, arriving just before dawn offers a great ride, even in the summer.

A great place to take your first ride here is in the northwest corner, just north of SR-50. Take exit #301 from I-75 and head east on SR-50. After crossing US-301 there are north and south entrances at 1, 3 and 5 miles past 301. East and west entrances are off of CR-471 which heads south from SR-50 at Tarrytown. These 471 access points are at the following appx. mileages south from SR-50: 2.2, 3.6, 5, 6.4 and 7.

Contacts: To obtain maps and information (like hunt dates) contact: Withlacoochee Forestry Center, 15019 Broad St., Brooksville, FL 34601, (352) 754-6777/ 6896. On the web: www.fl-dof.com ; Hunting schedules can be obtained from the Florida Fish & Wildlife Conservation Commission, 620 S. Meridian St., Tallahassee, FL 32399, (850) 488-4676 or (352) 732-1225. On the web: www.state.fl.us/fwc

Chassahowitzka Wildlife Management Area

Location: Between Weeki Wachee and Homosassa Springs

Managing Agency: U.S. Fish and Wildlife Service and Florida Fish and Wildlife Conservation Commission (FF&WCC).

Trail Length: 22.8 miles

Difficulty: 50% beginner; 50% intermediate

Trail Type: 100% doubletrack

Description: Sunny, scenic wilderness in the sandy uplands changes into a dark, wet, mysterious swamp, as you pedal into Chassahowitzka Wildlife Management Area. All of the doubletrack roads are earthen and approximately half are improved, hard pack roads offering relatively smooth surfaces of either lime rock or gravel. These are easy to ride, even for novice cyclists. The other half of the trails offer a more challenging ride with some sandy sections in the uplands and off-shoot trails into the hardwood swamp. These require constant rider attention to the immediate path ahead. Official vehicles occasionally travel here and have left deep ruts where their tires sank into the soft surface. If these little craters are full of water, avoid riding through them as some are quite deep with soft muck in the bottom. Even if you skirt the ruts by riding in between or around them, you still need to exercise caution: cypress knees have grown in the grass here. Bush-hogging has cut the tops off of most of these knees leaving barely visible, four inch stumps that can immediately stop a bicycle front wheel.

After these warnings, why would you want to ride here? Being able to see the primitive wilderness of a Florida hardwood swamp makes a trip here worthwhile. The off-shoot spur trails, which once served as tram roads for extracting timber, now offer an excellent venue deep into a swamp where most humans would not otherwise venture. While the old growth cypress and other hard woods were harvested more than 50 years ago, the more recent growth is mature, dense and tall. When entering a swamp spur trail you will be enshrouded in a tunnel of tree branches entwined above you. Narrow shafts of light seep through the forest canopy creating a spooky, foreboding appearance that lends enchantment to the thick swamp. Unless you are very quiet, many more pairs of eyes will watch you than you them. Numerous, large golden-orb spiders spin their webs across the trails and lurk in the center of concentric circles awaiting hapless victims much smaller than you. Be kind to them. It is not only the law to not harm wildlife, moreover, these spiders eat mosquitoes. Thus, they grew large being your friends.

Because the spurs from the main trail do not loop, riding out and back on all of them will add about 8 miles of riding to the 22.8 miles of trails. If you don't have the time or inclination to ride all of them, be sure to at least include one of the longer spurs in the Blind Creek area. This is an awesome area seen by very few.

The upland areas along the improved roads are less shady and more open, offering greater sight distance through oak and pine. Palmettos abound in these sandy, dry soils.

Wildlife: Because hunting is permitted during certain seasons on this tract, wildlife are somewhat reclusive. Whitetail deer, black bear, feral hog, gray squirrel, fox squirrel, rabbit, raccoon, opossum, skunk, coyote, beaver, nutria, armadillo, gopher tortoise, alligator, snakes, and wild turkey make their homes here. Many other bird species, including wading and migratory birds are also common.

Et cetera: Size: 29,729 acres. Hernando County. Avoid riding here during hunting season. Hunters are required to wear at least 500 square inches of daylight fluorescent-orange material above the waistline as an outer garment. If you plan to ride near hunting dates, be sure to do likewise. Hunt schedules vary slightly from year to year so call for the current details. Generally, archery season is mid-September through mid-October. Late October is muzzle-loading gun season and general gun runs from mid-November through mid-January. Day use permits, requiring a small fee, must be purchased at the trailhead on your left, about half a mile west of US-19. Bring your camera, lots of water and bug repellant. To discourage chiggers apply repellent to your feet beneath your socks and put some on your socks as well. Insects are less of a problem from December through February.

When to Go: Your experience will be more enjoyable September through May. If possible, avoid the hunting seasons noted in "Et cetera" above.

Contacts: Florida Fish & Wildlife Conservation Commission, 620 S. Meridian St., Tallahassee, FL 32399, (850) 488-4676. On the web at: www.state.fl.us/fwc

Directions: From Weeki Wachee at US-19 and SR-50 go approximately 10.5 miles north on US-19. Look for entrance on your left following brown highway sign noting the "Chassahowitzka Wildlife Management Area." Driving south from Homosassa Springs on US-19, a similar sign will be on your right about three miles south of the intersection of US-98.

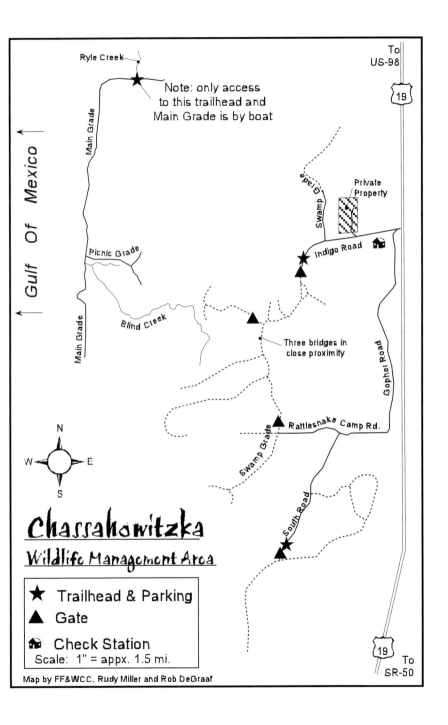

Ryle Creek

Note: only access to this trailhead and Main Grade is by boat

Main Grade

Gulf Of Mexico

Picnic Grade

Blind Creek

Main Grade

To US-98

19

Swamp Grade

Private Property

Indigo Road

Gopher Road

Three bridges in close proximity

Rattlesnake Camp Rd.

Swamp Grade

South Road

N
W — E
S

Chassahowitzka
Wildlife Management Area

★   Trailhead & Parking

▲   Gate

🏠   Check Station

Scale: 1" = appx. 1.5 mi.

Map by FF&WCC, Rudy Miller and Rob DeGraaf

19
To SR-50

Green Swamp Wilderness Preserve

Location: East of Dade City

Managing Agency: Southwest Florida Water Management District (SWFWMD), Florida Fish and Wildlife Conservation Commission (FF&WCC), and Florida Department of Environmental Protection, Division of Recreation and Parks.

Trail Length: East side 58 miles, West side 42 miles

Difficulty: Depends on distance ridden. East side is easier and OK for beginners through advanced. West side is best for intermediate to advanced.

Trail Type: 100% doubletrack

Description: Green Swamp is divided into two primary management units: Green Swamp West (GSW) is west of CR-471while Green Swamp East (GSE) is east of 471. The GSE trails are more rider friendly: they have a mostly hard pack surface with just a few sandy sections during the drier months and some wet sections after heavy rainfall. By comparison, GSW trails are shared by equestrians and are often in deep sand or tall grass making them more difficult to ride. Much of GSW was ranch land in the recent past, thus giving it a pasture like look. This also makes much of the terrain a bit drier than GSE. If you have several days to ride, the authors suggest riding the east side first, then if time remains, go check out GSW. In GSE, Main Grade has the best riding surface and trails from here are quite predictable. As you leave one trail and turn onto another, the initial surface condition of the new trail is a great indicator of what's to come.

The Green Swamp is aptly named. Because of the abundant and vast stretches of water, the swamp rarely freezes. Because of all the water, most vegetation is "green" throughout the year. Shallow water lies on both sides of the trails in most sections helping to define the "swamp" aspect of its name. The area is a complex mosaic of disturbed uplands and wetlands intermixed with higher quality swamps. It is estimated that 90% of the native upland vegetation in the entire, 560,000 acre Green Swamp has been disturbed by agriculture and development. Much of this damage was caused in the early 1900's by excessive logging of cypress and other timber. Development and destruction of other portions of the swamp over the years has also left a dent in the ecosystem's fragile armor. Of the 560,000 acres comprising the original swamp, 110,000 acres currently lie within the Preserve and thus in public ownership. This preservation effort was spearheaded in 1968 by the Southwest Florida Water Management District. New parcels continue to be added (by various agencies) to this vast and ecologically vital network comprising the Green Swamp. All of this land acquisition comes at a hefty price: the estimated assessed tax value of Green Swamp currently exceeds $140,000,000. You and I own the land so ride and enjoy!

When one thinks of wet areas like swamps, one usually thinks of lands which are very low in elevation. Well, they usually are. However, Green Swamp is an oddity: it is actually higher than areas lying well outside its confines. Think of it as a huge, elevated, natural reservoir surrounded by high, sandy ridges impounding the water within. How then does it gather this quantity of water? Most of it comes from rainfall. In an area this large, in the summer, it's a good bet that it is raining at least somewhere on the property! This accumulated rainfall collects in the swamp and flows across the surface in various directions creating the headwaters to four major rivers: the Withlacoochee, Ocklawaha, Peace, and the Hillsborough. This water, due to the swamp's incredibly high groundwater elevation (the highest in the peninsula), also serves as a vital water recharge zone for the Floridan Aquifer.

<u>Wildlife:</u> Whitetail deer, feral hog, myriad snakes, wild turkey, many species of

Photo by Jean Miller
Rudy Miller takes in the scenery at Green Swamp

wading birds, birds of prey (e.g., red shouldered hawk, owls, etc.) can be found here. Wood stork, scrub jay, gopher tortoise and other protected species are on the property. Wildlife, while plentiful, are accustomed to being hunted annually so they tend to stay out of site unless you ride during dawn or dusk hours and do so quietly. Mosquitos breed well in a swamp and some of these are the size of wasps. Applying repellant liberally and often should allow you to give your attention to the beautiful scenery, wildflowers and butterflies.

<u>Et cetera:</u> Size: GSE = 67,670 acres and GSW = 37,350 acres. Lake, Pasco, Polk and Sumter Counties. Hours: sunrise to sunset. Call contact number listed below to obtain a current trail map of the property. Ride only on trails marked for bicycles. Bring plenty of water (several bottles and/or a hydration pack), food, insect repellant and sun screen, and use each frequently. Dehydration can occur rapidly in the summer. A map, compass and GPS (if available) are recommended as is a first-aid kit; know how to use each. Also bring a couple of spare tubes, a pump and any vital tools. This is a wild area encompassing thousands of acres so be prepared. One of the authors incurred a 4 day long stay in the hospital from a little too much Green Swamp adventure in summer '98. . . . Avoid hunt season days which are scattered from September through April. Obtain a current hunt schedule for exact dates. Note: scheduled hunt dates vary between GSE and GSW. Primitive campsites are available. Thirty-six miles of the scenic Withlacoochee River meander through the Preserve making for great paddling trips.

The Lanier bridge at River Road is a good put in point for trips downstream (and upstream when there's enough water). Nearby Withlacoochee River Park offers good hiking and a nice lookout tower. Near the River Road bridge, head south following signs.

When to Go: By far, the cooler months are the best time to ride, however, this is also hunt season so be sure to obtain current hunt dates before heading out. Summer rides are brutally hot and equally humid. Ride dawn or dusk only to avoid mid-day temperatures.

Contacts: Southwest Florida Water Management District, Land Resources Department, 2379 Broad St., Brooksville, FL 34604, (800) 423-1476 ext. 4470. On the web: www.swfwmd.state.fl.us ; Florida Fish & Wildlife Conservation Commission, 620 S. Meridian St., Tallahassee, FL 32399, (850) 488-4676 or (352) 732-1225. On the web: www.state.fl.us/fwc

Directions: There are over a half dozen trailheads into Green Swamp. This does not include secondary bike-through gates. Directions are provided here to the major trailheads into both GSE and GSW. . . . The first two trailheads, located on CR-471, afford access to GSE and GSW from the same points. The more southern of the two is located where the Withlacoochee River passes under 471. This is appx. 4 mi. north of US-98. The second, more northern of the two is located appx. 6 mi. north of US-98 at Cumpressco Road. . . To reach the west entrance into GSW, take River Road east from US-301 in Dade City. Continue heading east, cross the Lanier Bridge (over the Withlacoochee River), and find entrance at gate straight ahead. . . Several trailheads provide access into GSE from the south. The main one, affording closer access to more trails, is reached from US-98. Either from the north or south on US-98, turn east onto Rock Ridge Rd. (traffic light here). In appx. 5 ½ miles, bear left to stay on Rock Ridge Rd. Head another 5 miles or so and look for main entrance on left. . . Other southern access into GSE is at trailhead on north side of US-98, appx. 4 mi. south of CR-54 and appx. 2 mi. north of Rock Ridge Rd. I remember an old forest tower being located there but it may be gone by time of printing. The trail from here heads several miles due north into GSE before reaching other trails and the Withlacoochee River. . . Another good trailhead for those wanting a far east entry is accessed from SR-33 in Lake County. Appx. 6 mi. south of SR-50 and appx. 7 mi. north of the Lake/ Polk County line, look for Lake Erie Rd. It heads west from SR-33. Follow it several miles west then make a left onto Bay Lake Rd. Follow this to parking signs for the Van Fleet State Rail Trail. One can bike west from here on dirt roads into the Little Withlacoochee Flood Detention Area, continue west into the Richloam Tract of the Withlacoochee SF or head south into GSE. Note: this is a more remote, lesser used trailhead than others listed above and this side of property is lightly visited/ monitored so caution and good planning are advised.

Upper Hillsborough Wildlife Management Area

Location: East of Zephyrhills

Managing Agency: Southwest Florida Water Management District (SWFWMD), and Florida Fish and Wildlife Conservation Commission (FF&WCC)

Trail Length: Appx. 12 miles

Difficulty: Easy but depends on speed and length of stay. Northern trails are more rugged

Trail Type: 100% doubletrack

Description: Wild and semi-remote, Upper Hillsborough is an ecologically significant property that, along with the Green Swamp, provides natural flood control and water recharge for the Hillsborough River. Moreover, it provides an invaluable wildlife corridor, or greenway, along the river connecting the Green Swamp with southern parcels in Tampa (e.g., Lower Hillsborough Wilderness Park).

Bicycling here should be a well-planned occasion. Most trails are not marked. Several off shoots leave mapped trails and dead end unexpectedly at wetlands, fence lines, etc. Bring a compass or a GPS and pay close attention to items listed below in the Et Cetera section! There are typically no rangers or staff on the property.

Trails here include hardpack, doubletrack, dirt roads leading through thickly vegetated woods with plenty of shade. A few sugar-sand roads are in the south but these can usually be avoided with other routes. There are three main sections, slightly separated by CR-54 in one instance and by the CSX Railroad in another (see map). In general, these sections become more rugged and wild as you head north due to much less visitation in that area. Trailheads in the northern section are especially difficult to find. Gates are somewhat over vegetated due to minimal usage and trails are very rugged, overgrown, and frequently rooted by feral hogs and armadillos. These are conditions that make biking sluggish at best. Yet, the north is among the most scenic sections of the property.

With this many trailheads there are many ride options: loops, out-and-backs, long one-ways using two vehicles, etc. I have ridden from the Chancey Road gate, east on Cedar Ford, NW along the railroad track, then over the railroad track into the central section, out onto 54 for ½ mile east before heading north into the uppermost section.

Flat Ford Road is worth mentioning. In one section, the trail parallels the railroad track on the south as it crosses the river. The bridge structure itself is somewhat unique. This section also affords a rare glimpse of an extreme upper section of the Hillsborough River flood plain: so far north in fact that the river is often dry here. During periods of wet weather, the Green Swamp, lying to the north, overflows. This feeds the Withlacoochee River, which then overflows its swampy banks in the south and feeds the uppermost portion of the Hillsborough River. The overall connectivity of the Green Swamp with several central Florida rivers, including the

Hillsborough, is a very interesting phenomenon.

Proper planning and good navigating skills can make for an adventurous and rewarding ride. Take time to appreciate the surrounding environment. Bring a lunch, spend the day. Take pictures but leave only bike tracks.

<u>Wildlife:</u> Whitetail deer, turkey, gopher tortoise, feral hog, armadillo, and myriad birds especially in wetter sections. Flora consists of slash and longleaf pine flatwoods, palmetto and gallberry understory, oaks in uplands and bald cypress in wetland areas.

<u>Et cetera:</u> Size: 9,961 acres. Pasco and Polk Counties. Hours: sunrise to sunset. Bring plenty of food and water (several bottles and/ or a hydration pack). A map and compass are recommended as is a first-aid kit; know how to use each. Also bring a couple of spare tubes, a pump and any vital tools. This is a wild area encompassing thousands of acres so be prepared. There is no bridge where Cedar Ford Road crosses the Hillsborough River. In the dry season this is not a problem. However, in the summer or after periods of heavy rain, wading this section may be necessary. Do not cross river if too deep. Safer, more suitable routes exist. Hunting is permitted on southern and central sections. Call FF&WCC for hunt dates. Typically in winter months. During hunts, vehicles are permitted on most woods roads. An off-shoot of the Florida Trail can be hiked on the property.

<u>When to Go:</u> Fall, winter, and spring are the most enjoyable seasons to bike here, as they are cooler and drier.

Rebecca Tharrington finishing up a long ride at Upper Hillsborough   *Photo by Rob DeGraaf*

Contacts: Southwest Florida Water Management District, 2379 Broad Street, Brooksville, FL 34604, (800) 423-1476. On the web: www.swfwmd.state.fl.us ; For hunt information and dates contact: Florida Fish & Wildlife Conservation Commission, 620 S. Meridian St., Tallahassee, FL 32399, (850) 488-4676. On the web: www.state.fl.us/fwc

Directions: Several trailheads (see map). Two main ones being CR-54 and Chancey Road. CR-54 trailhead is located appx. 4 miles east of US-301 in Zephyrhills. Make a right heading south, on west side of railroad tracks. Follow dirt road to parking area. . . . Chancey Road (CR-535) trailhead is somewhat harder to find. Chancey Road intersects several roads in Zephyrhills. From US-301 in Zephyrhills, take CR-54 east appx. 3 miles. Make right heading south onto Chancey Road. Drive appx. 2 1/4 miles and look for gate on east side of road. Gate will appear just after Chancey Road begins to bend. Room for only a few vehicles here. See map for other trailheads but note that these are bike/ walk through only. No parking permitted.

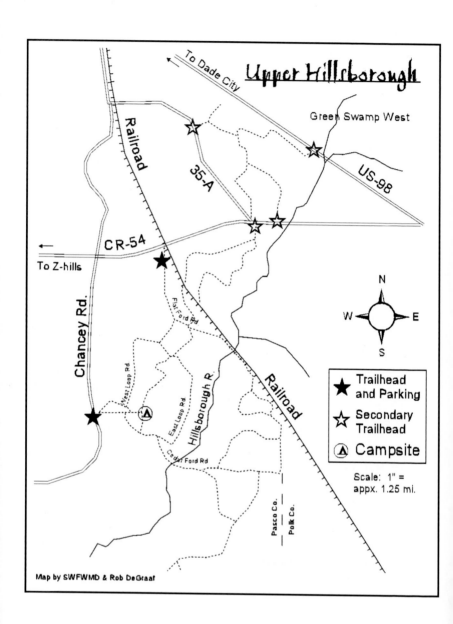

Upper Hillsborough

Green Swamp West

To Dade City

Railroad

35-A

US-98

CR-54

To Z-hills

Chancey Rd.

Flat Ford Rd

West Loop Rd

East Loop Rd

Hillsborough R.

Cedar Ford Rd

Railroad

N
W   E
S

★ Trailhead
and Parking

☆ Secondary
Trailhead

Ⓐ Campsite

Scale: 1" =
appx. 1.25 mi.

Pasco Co.
Polk Co.

Map by SWFWMD & Rob DeGraaf

Dead River Park - Hillsborough River State Park

Location: Both parks on US-301, north of Tampa, near Thonotosassa

Managing Agency: Hillsborough County Parks and Recreation Department and Florida Department of Environmental Protection, Division of Recreation and Parks

Trail Length: Appx. 10 to 11 miles round trip

Difficulty: Easy

Trail Type: 50% singletrack; 50% doubletrack and dirt roads

Description: Pedaling down a virtually empty trail in Dead River Park, paralleling the Hillsborough River, I looked up in response to strange cries from above. A mating pair of sand hill cranes were circling in the firmament, bellowing like raspy, Model-T horns. Sharing the skies with the cranes were a beautiful pair of red-shouldered hawks. Sightings like these are somewhat common along the Hillsborough River watershed.

Owned by the Southwest Florida Water Management District and managed by the county, Dead River Park is just one park in a group of many comprising what is known as Lower Hillsborough Wilderness Park. The site is not well known, thus not heavily visited. Most come here to fish or take in a leisurely stroll along the river. Scenery is top notch, featuring well canopied, narrow, hardpack trails and double-track roads with several great views of the river. Cypress, oak, magnolia, hickory and other trees adorn the riverside trails and hardwood swamp terrain. The gravel entrance road is worth a look by itself as it is fully canopied, lined with cypress and huge grandfather oak trees laden with resurrection fern. Along the way, scan the thick woods on your left for an old tractor. The gravel road actually makes a nicer bike ride than vehicle drive! Just be cautious as you will be "sharing" the road. Note: when riding here, be courteous by yielding trail to hikers. Several blind turns exist. See below for ride suggestions.

Compared to Dead River, Hillsborough River State Park is well known. This may in part be due to the park being among the oldest in the state, having opened in 1938 thanks to development by the Civilian Conservation Corps. At almost 3,000 acres, the park boasts many recreational and cultural activities (listed below). Entering the park, you will pass through upland forest consisting of mostly slash pine/ palmetto community. Closer to the river, hardwoods predominate: oak, cypress, hickory, magnolia, etc. The off-road bike trail starts from the Wetland Restoration Trail parking area, located almost all the way around the main park road, on the right.

Ride suggestions:

1. Park at Hillsborough River State Park, Wetlands Restoration Trailhead. Begin by heading south from here. Make first main right onto well worn dirt road, heading west. This leads through a somewhat open, county owned parcel, then continues along an old doubletrack tram road. Bike through the opening near gate. You

are now in Dead River Park. This trail leads to Dead River trailhead and gravel road which in turn leads to US-301. Small loop trail near Dead River Group Camp is an option (adds ½ mile) as is an out and back on gravel road (adds 4 miles).

2. Park at Dead River main gate (where paved road ends). Follow road 2 miles to river then either make left to ride ½ mile loop trail near camp or make right to head toward Hillsborough River SP, or do both! To get to state park, follow river trail, pass through gate, cross county property, then make left onto doubletrack dirt road leading to Wetland Restoration Trailhead.

3. When park is open (see hours below), park at main trailhead at river then either head south to ride ½ mile loop trail near camp, head north along river trail, or do both. To get to state park, follow directions in #2 above. Notes: using map will facilitate navigation. To add an additional 2 miles to any of the above rides, follow the paved road loop within Hillsborough River State Park.

Wildlife: Whitetail deer, red fox, feral hog, armadillo, raccoon, opossum, turkey, endangered gopher tortoise, eastern diamond-back rattlesnake, cottonmouth, yellow-rat snake, alligator, river otter, limpkin, ibis, egret, various heron, roseate spoonbill, sand hill crane, red-shouldered hawk, etc. One day I was lucky enough to observe a river otter playing in the rapids, taking an occasional break on exposed limestone rocks in river. Trees & plants include live oak, scrub oak, bald cypress, slash pine, magnolia, hickory, cedar, cabbage palm, saw palmetto, boston fern, resurrection fern, string fern, etc.

Et cetera: Size: Dead River = 21 acres. HRSP = 3414 acres. Hillsborough County. Park hours for Dead River Park are: 9 am to 5:30 pm, Friday, Saturday & Sunday. Gate closed Monday thru Thursday. Hours for Hillsborough River State Park: 8 am to sunset, year round. Bring plenty of food and water (several bottles and/ or a hydration pack). A map and compass are recommended as is a first-aid kit; know how to use each. Also bring a couple of spare tubes, a pump, any vital tools, a lightweight rain-coat, and insect repellent. Small entrance fee to drive into Hillsborough River State Park.

Other opportunities include: Hillsborough River SP: hiking on trails and boardwalks, canoeing/ kayaking, fishing, nature study, camping, picnicking, swimming in ½ acre pool, touring 1830's Ft. Foster Historic Site. The Hillsborough river is incredibly scenic and is a highly suggested canoe/ kayak trip. A hike down the Rapids Trail is a must! Here the river takes a rare plunge over exposed Suwannee limestone creating, in high water, one of Florida's only class-II rapids. Dead River Park: hiking, fishing, nature study, canoeing/ kayaking, picnicking, and camping at group camp with advance reservations.

The Fort King Greenway trail is in the planning stages. It will connect these parks along with others (e.g., Sargent Park), along the Hillsborough River. Much of mileage will make use of historical right-of-way from old Ft. King Highway. Food can be found in Tampa, Zephyrhills, or by following 301 south to McIntosh Rd. Make left heading south several miles to Knight's Griffin Rd. Restaurant is at intersection of McIntosh and Knight's Griffin.

When to Go: Fall, winter, and spring are the most enjoyable seasons to bike here, as they are cooler and much drier. However, trails drain quickly in summer and most of the route is shaded.

Contacts: For Dead River Park: Hillsborough County Parks and Recreation Department: (813) 975-2160; For Hillsborough River State Park: 15402 US-301 North, Thonotosassa, FL 33592. (813) 987-6771.

Directions: To Dead River Park: From Tampa take Fowler Ave. east to US-301. Make a left heading north. Dead River Rd. will fork off to the left at appx. 8 to 9 miles from Fowler Ave. Follow road to gate. Choose whether to park here (to add appx. 4 miles to ride) or drive to main trailhead near river. To Hillsborough River State Park: follow same general directions from Tampa above. From Fowler, drive appx. 10 to 11 miles before making left into park. Pay entrance fee. Driving almost completely around the paved loop road, you will come to the Wetland Restoration Trailhead on right.

Thickly canopied river trail at Dead River Park   *Photo by Rob DeGraaf*

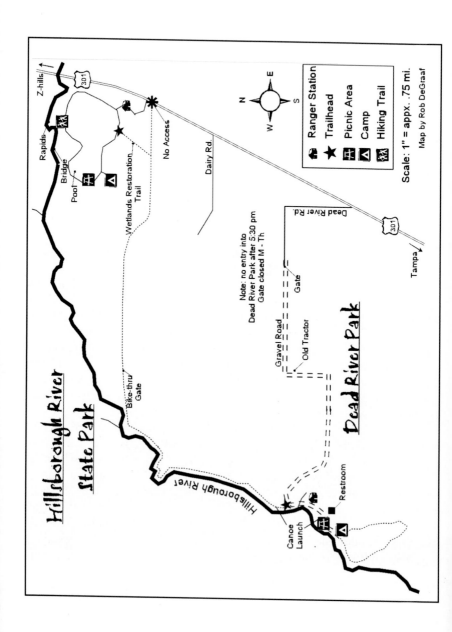

Hillsborough River
State Park

Dead River Park

Hillsborough River

Z-hills
Rapids
Bridge
Pool
Wetlands Restoration Trail
No Access
Dairy Rd.
Bike-thru Gate
Canoe Launch
Restroom
301

Note: no entry into Dead River Park after 5:30 pm
Gate closed M - Th

Gravel Road
Old Tractor
Gate
Dead River Rd.
301
Tampa

Legend:
- Ranger Station
- ★ Trailhead
- Picnic Area
- ▲ Camp
- Hiking Trail

Scale: 1" = appx. .75 mi.

Map by Rob DeGraaf

N W E S

122

Tenoroc Fish Management Area

Location: Northeast of Lakeland

Managing Agency: Florida Fish and Wildlife Conservation Commission, Polk County Board of County Commissioners, and Division of Forestry

Trail Length: Appx. 19 miles

Difficulty: 70% beginner; 25% intermediate; 5% advanced

Trail Type: 30% singletrack; 70% doubletrack and dirt roads

Description: I know what you're thinking: "What decent biking could there be at a Fish Management Area?" The answer is, LOTS, and maybe more to come in the near future. While the recreational focus at Tenoroc is unarguably fishing, there is lots of very lightly visited woodsy acreage on the property. And, much of this is scattered with large dirt mounds and ridges (tailings) left over from the park's days of phosphate mining which ended in the mid-seventies. Coronet (spelled backwards is TENOROC) Industries had mining rights of the property for a duration, and in 1982, land owner, Borden, Inc. donated the land to the state for conservation purposes.

The park is receptive to permitting a separately designated mountain-bike trail and at the time of writing, this option was being discussed between me and the Lakeland based Ridge Riders Mountain Bike Association (RRMBA). If things work out, more of the "currently unrealized" hilly terrain could be incorporated into a premier mountain-biking venue potentially rivaling other local mountain-biking areas.

The property's lakes help fulfill the "wet dreams" of local fishermen. Tailings and other hilly, old mining terrain, will likely have the same effect on off-road bicyclists. Interestingly, the tailings are the result of the creation of the lakes. This, at least here, makes bicycling and fishing close cousins.

Beginning at the Picnic Lake trailhead, the 2 ½ mile long Blue Trail heads into the woods then exits before coming out to the main park road (gravel at this point). Two choices exist here: 1. Follow the dirt road. This is straight and flat and leads to Collins Cemetery and beyond. 2. Cross the dirt road and walk over a log bridge, then re-enter the woods. The latter choice is singletrack. Both routes (1 and 2) will get you to the same area (see map).

Choice 2 leads to a small creek, crossed via an angled bridge which drops off abruptly on the other side. The drop is appx. 1 ½ feet here and will either give fright or delight to riders depending on their skill level. Just when you thought the excitement was over, next comes a steep ridge climb. Once reaching the top, cyclists are rewarded with a very panoramic view of the surrounding woods.

The first time I climbed this ridge, I saw something that surprised me. A huge soft-shelled tortoise was sitting atop the hill, just off the trail, soaking up the midday sun. The closest water was around 50 feet below. My friend and I stared in amazement. We had heard the expression, "like a fish out of water" but had never needed to apply it to a turtle . . . until now that was. After a few minutes, the turtle became shy and decided it was time to head south. He or she slid down the steep hill in what seemed like reckless abandon, demonstrating very un-turtle like speed. Plants could be heard crashing and then, finally, the noise stopped and the turtle could be seen at the water's edge. Thoughts of downhill riding, through narrow, twisty lines (like the turtle's) mysteriously entered my head. . . .

The Blue Trail continues along the ridge for a while before heading downhill into more open terrain where it joins the 2.9 mile long Orange Trail. This trail is mostly flat, straight doubletrack but does include a relatively short singletrack stretch in the south. The Orange Trail forms a loop heading to the south then back north again. Look for wild blackberry bushes on Blue Trail near juncture with Orange Trail.

Fifteen miles of lightly used horseback trail are open to off-road bicyclists here. Two loops, one in north and one in south, begin just west of the main park office. It is very rare to see shared horseback/ off-road bicycling trail in Florida. Usually, sandy conditions common in Florida preclude enjoyable bicycling on said trails. Tenoroc is different, being that the trail surfaces are mostly clay. Cyclists must yield trail to horseback riders! This is their trail first, ours by luck. In passing horses, engage riders in trail side conversation. This helps calm anxious, wary horses.

Wildlife: Feral hog, armadillo, raccoon, opossum, turkey, endangered gopher tortoise, soft-shelled tortoise, alligator, and myriad birds including osprey, red-shouldered hawk, woodpecker, great blue heron, ibis, etc. Trees and plants include live oak, slash pine, occasional cedar, cabbage palm, jacaranda, Brazilian pepper, palmetto, boston fern, wild blackberry, lantana, caesar's weed and muscadine grape.

Et cetera: Size: appx. 7,000 acres. Polk County. Helmet required. Entrance fee required. Bring plenty of food and water (several bottles and/ or a hydration pack). A map and compass are recommended as is a first-aid kit; know how to use each. Also bring a couple of spare tubes, a pump, any vital tools, a lightweight raincoat, and insect repellent. Hiking and Horseback riding shared on trails listed here. Fishing is priority number one here. Many lakes and access points to choose from. Gun and archery ranges also on property.

When to Go: Fall, winter, and spring are the most enjoyable seasons to bike here, as they are cooler and much drier. Most trails here drain quickly after rainfall. Call the park for hours of operation before heading out.

Contacts: Tenoroc Fish Management Area, 3829 Tenoroc Mine Road, Lakeland, FL 33805, (863) 499-2422

Directions: Best access is from I-4. Exit #38. Take SR-33 south appx. 1 ½ miles then bear left onto Combee Road (SR-659). Head south just over a mile then make left onto Tenoroc Mine Road. Follow road to park HQ. Pay entrance fee and register. Continue heading east to Picnic Lake parking area (on your left). Blue Trail starts here and connects to Orange Trail 2.5 miles in. Horse trails (open to bikes) begin on west side of park HQ and head north and south from here forming two separate loops.

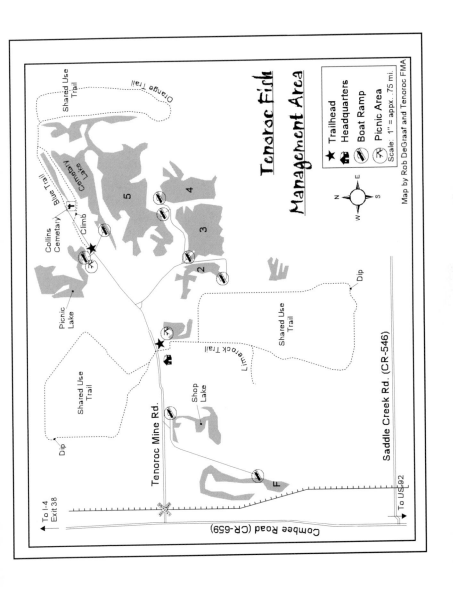

Tenoroc Fish Management Area

Map by Rob DeGraaf and Tenoroc FMA

★ Trailhead
Headquarters
Boat Ramp
Picnic Area
Scale: 1" = appx. .75 mi.

Avon Park Air Force Range

Location: East of Avon Park, north of Sebring

Managing Agency: U.S. Air Force and Florida Fish and Wildlife Conservation Commission

Trail Length: Roughly 200 miles

Difficulty: Depends on speed and length of stay

Trail Type: Doubletrack and other dirt roads

Description: "If God did not make it, leave it alone." This phrase applies to any government property found at Avon Park. Unexploded munitions and dangerous phosphorous flares should not be touched or tampered with. If possible, mark their location then contact the Natural Resources Office about the object(s).

The opening phrase also congers up memories of my days spent in Air Force basic training. Just to keep us new recruits constantly busy, we were often sent on base cleanup duty. Conversely to the above, we were always told, "Unless it's growing there, pick it up." This even applied to rocks which after collection were then re-scattered in fields for the next group of recruits. At any rate, the point is that you have to leave things as you find them at Avon Park. When speaking about potential unspent munitions, this shouldn't be too hard to do!

If you think this property is big now, you should have been here during WW-II when it was three times larger. Back then, its northern boundary stretched all the way to Lake Kissimmee. Much of the same training taking place back then is still performed today. Aircraft drop practice bombs in designated, well marked-off ranges. These ranges are bordered by buffering management units that are closed off during missions. These same units are open when missions are not being flown, however, the ranges themselves are NEVER open for recreation. This is a good thing.

For the most part, every paved or dirt road on the property open to vehicles is open to bicyclists. Most of these, even the paved roads, are very lightly traveled. In addition to this, the 12 mile segment of the Florida National Scenic Trail (FNST) is open to off-road bicyclists. This is a rare treat since most of the FNST statewide is closed to bicyclists at present. Constructed by hikers of the Florida Trail Association, bicyclists should act courteously by yielding trail to hikers when on the FNST. The trail is very lightly used as evidenced by lack of a true worn path of any sort. Navigation must then be accomplished by following orange blazes on trees; hope your eyesight is good. The FNST winds through the most exemplary hardwood hammock on the Range, paralleling the scenic Kissimmee River to the east. The trail, being so lightly used, is slow and rugged but exceptionally scenic. It can be accessed in several locations: Orange Hammock Road in the north, Kissimmee Road midway, and Tank Trail in the south (if this portion is open). It should also be noted that the Range can be entered or exited via the FNST. To the north, KICCO is also open to off-road bicycling. To the south, Boney Marsh is not.

The Arbuckle Marsh Dike is an elevated trail leading through open marsh. It is closed to vehicles. Ride here during cooler weather as there is no shade. The trail is most easily accessed from the southern end of Ebersbach Rd. Bikes and bodies must cross over the gate. Other access lies further south at Johnston Rd. This area is very remote and is prone to flooding during wet weather. Ask Range staff for most current conditions. An interesting loop can be ridden by combining the Dike trail with various roads to the north, east and south. This loop would be appx. 20 miles in length.

To plan a "successful" trip here:

1. Call the Ranger to see if open for the weekend and to see if certain portions are scheduled to be closed for military exercises. (Note: the Range is open to the public for recreation from noon Thursday to 8:00 p.m. Monday. Closed all day Tuesday and Wednesday). While on the phone, be sure to specify that you're coming to bike! Staff sometimes think of "recreation" as only hunting, thus biking may not be allowed at that time.

2. Check in at the Outdoor Recreation building (ask for directions at main gate).

3. Pay entrance fee, sign waiver and obtain safety briefing.

4. Ask for Public Recreation Area Map and Natural Resources Interpretive Guide.

5. Make sure you have necessary provisions (water, food, gas, etc.) at this point before heading into the Range from here.

Outdoor Recreation staff are knowledgeable of current conditions of roads, trails and management units. Inquire within before heading out. In dry weather, some roads can become pure sugar sand. In general, these conditions improve with summer rains. Trails that are not open to bicyclists include the Lake Arbuckle National Recreation Trail (in NE of Range) and the hiking trail in Sandy Point Wildlife Refuge. However, if time permits these should be explored by foot.

<u>Wildlife:</u> Many ecosystems (several endangered) combine on the property to represent a fairly holistic sampling of south-central Florida habitat in general. Ask Outdoor Recreation for the "Natural Resources Interpretive Guide." This guide lists most of the flora, fauna and ecosystems found on the Range. It also contains a cool, color-coded map depicting plant communities and other information.

<u>Et cetera:</u> Size: 106,000 acres. 82,000 acres open for public recreation. Highlands and Polk Counties. Park entrance fee and permit required. Bring plenty of food and water (several bottles and/ or a hydration pack). A map, compass and GPS (if available) are recommended as is a first-aid kit; know how to use each. Also bring a couple of spare tubes, a pump and any vital tools. Insect repellent, sun screen and rain gear also suggested. This is a wild area encompassing thousands of acres so be prepared. Ticks and chiggers may be a problem, so load up on insect repellent before heading out. Post ride, be sure to check for ticks. Other Range activities include camping, hiking, horseback riding, fishing and hunting. A cool, old lookout tower is located ½ mile up Old Bravo Road from Kissimmee Road. In general, hunt dates run from late Oct. - early Nov., then from mid Nov. to late Dec. Call for exact dates. Many options for food and lodging can be found along US-27. El Zarape III, east of 27 on Main St., Avon Park, serves up Mexican food. The Cat House in down-

town Sebring is a quirky restaurant geared toward the feline fanatic. Historic Kenilworth Lodge in downtown Sebring caters to cyclists! They're used to us sweaty, dirty gear heads and will even store your bikes in a locked room upon request.

When to Go: Make sure the Range is open before heading out. At times, the entire property closes to the public for special military exercises. Fall, winter, and spring are the most enjoyable seasons to bike here, as they are cooler and drier. Summer heat can be brutal on certain wide open roads. In general, the Range is closed to recreationists from late October to late December for various hunts. Call for exact dates before heading out. An exception is the 12 mile segment of the Florida National Scenic Trail along the Kissimmee River, however, access through the Range may be questionable, so call before heading out.

Contacts: Avon Park Bomb Range, Natural Resource Manager, 56 CSS-DEN, 236 South Blvd., Avon Park AFB, FL 33825. Main number: (863) 452-4254. Pre-recorded information: (863) 452-4119 Ext. 5.

Directions: From US-27 in Avon Park. Take SR-64 (Main Street) east appx. 9 miles to main gate of Range. Ask for directions to the Outdoor Recreation Office from here. . .North (back) gate from Lake Arbuckle Road is only open during hunt season. Call the Range for exact dates and times.

References

Audubon Society. *Field Guide to North American Birds, Eastern Region.* Alfred A. Knopf, Inc. Most current edition used.

Bell, C. R., and B.J. Taylor. *Florida Wild Flowers and Roadside Plants.* Chapel Hill, NC: Laurel Hill Press, 1998.

DeLorme. *Florida Atlas & Gazetteer.* Freeport, ME: DeLorme. Most current edition used.

Florida Fish and Wildlife Conservation Commission. *What Have You Done for Wildlife Lately?* Tallahassee, FL: FF & WCC, 1995.

Larson, Ron. *Swamp Song: A Natural History of Florida's Swamps.* Gainesville, FL: University Press of Florida, 1995.

Martin, Bruce. *A Guide to All Terrain Biking in Central Florida.* Orlando, FL: Florida Freewheelers, Inc., 1998.

Morris, Joan Perry. *Florida Place Names.* Sarasota, FL: Pineapple Press, Inc., 1995.

Nelson, Gil. *The Trees of Florida: A Reference and Field Guide.* Sarasota, FL: Pineapple Press, Inc., 1994.

Perry, John, and Jane G. Perry. *The Sierra Club Guide to the Natural Areas of Florida.* San Francisco: Sierra Club Books, 1992.

South Florida Water Management District. *Public Use Guide for Designated Land Management Areas.* West Palm Beach: SFWMD. Most current edition used.

South Florida Water Management District. *Save Our Rivers: Five Year Plan.* West Palm Beach: SFWMD. Most current edition used.

Southwest Florida Water Management District. *Recreational Guide.* Brooksville, FL: SWFWMD 2001.

St. Johns River Water Management District. *Recreation Guide to Public Lands.* Palatka, FL: SJRWMD. Most current edition used.

Strutin, Michal. *Florida State Parks: A Complete Recreation Guide.* Seattle: The Mountaineers Books, 2000.

Trail Notes

Trail Notes

Trail Notes

Trail Notes

Trail Notes

Trail Notes

Trail Notes